839.726 S918zz M946
Mueller, Carl Richard
Strindberg in an hour

STRINDBERG

in an hour

Y0-AUZ-720

BY CARL R. MUELLER

WITHDRAWN

SUSAN C. MOORE, SERIES EDITOR

PLAYWRIGHTS in an hour
know the playwright, love the play

IN AN HOUR BOOKS • HANOVER, NEW HAMPSHIRE • INANHOURBOOKS.COM
AN IMPRINT OF SMITH AND KRAUS PUBLISHERS, INC • SMITHANDKRAUS.COM

CUYAHOGA COMMUNITY COLLEGE
EASTERN CAMPUS LIBRARY

With grateful thanks to Carl R. Mueller, whose fascinating introductions to his translations of the Greek and German playwrights provided inspiration for this series.

Published by In an Hour Books
an imprint of Smith and Kraus, Inc.
177 Lyme Road, Hanover, NH 03755
inanhourbooks.com SmithandKraus.com

Know the playwright, love the play.

In an Hour, In a Minute, and Theater IQ are registered trademarks of
In an Hour Books.

© 2009 by In an Hour Books
All rights reserved
Manufactured in the United States of America
First edition: April 2010
10 9 8 7 6 5 4 3 2 1

All rights reserved including the right of reproduction in whole or in
part in any form except for use in reviews of the book and/or series.
Please direct inquiries to In an Hour Books (603) 643-6431.

All scenes © 2002 by Carl R. Mueller. Reprinted by permission of Hugh
Denard, Executor of the estate of Carl R. Mueller. For performance rights,
contact Smith and Kraus, Inc. at licensing@smithandkraus.com
www.smithandkraus.com.

Front cover design by Dan Mehling, dmehling@gmail.com
Text design by Kate Mueller, Electric Dragon Productions
Book production by Dede Cummings Design, DCDesign@sover.net

ISBN-13: 978-1-936232-28-4
ISBN-10: 1-936232-28-6
Library of Congress Control Number: 2009943220

CONTENTS

Why Playwrights in an Hour?

This new series by Smith and Kraus Publishers titled Playwrights in an Hour has a dual purpose for being: one academic, the other general. For the general reader, this volume, as well as the many others in the series, offers in compact form the information needed for a basic understanding and appreciation of the works of each volume's featured playwright. Which is not to say that there don't exist volumes on end devoted to each playwright under consideration. But inasmuch as few are blessed with enough time to read the splendid scholarship that is available, a brief, highly focused accounting of the playwright's life and work is in order. The central feature of the series, a thirty- to forty-page essay, integrates the playwright into the context of his or her time and place. The volumes, though written to high standards of academic integrity, are accessible in style and approach to the general reader as well as to the student and, of course, to the theater professional and theatergoer. These books will serve for the brushing up of one's knowledge of a playwright's career, to the benefit of theater work or theatergoing. The Playwrights in an Hour series represents all periods of Western theater: Aeschylus to Shakespeare to Wedekind to Ibsen to Williams to Beckett, and on to the great contemporary playwrights who continue to offer joy and enlightenment to a grateful world.

Carl R. Mueller
School of Theater, Film and Television
Department of Theater
University of California, Los Angeles

Introduction

At first sight, August Strindberg would seem to be the most revolutionary spirit in modern theater. Through his own inflammatory writings, he had a deep influence on such later theatrical "incendiaries" as Antonin Artaud, Jean Genet, and Edward Albee. Though the distinction of chief revolutionary must go to Henrik Ibsen, Strindberg is certainly the more restless and experimental figure. Perpetually dissatisfied, always reaching after shifting truths, he is a latter-day Faust with the unconscious as his laboratory, seeking the miracle of transmutation in the crucible of his tormented intellect.

The metaphor has not been carelessly chosen — the conversion of baser material into something higher, through the philosopher's stone of imagination, is the goal of all his activity, whether dramatic or non-dramatic. Strindberg not only tries his hand at a great variety of dramatic styles, he commits himself to a great variety of religious and political creeds. His literary work is one long autobiography, whether in the form of confessional novels, misogynistic short stories, revolutionary verses, scientific treatises, theatrical manifestoes, or short plays. More than any other dramatist in history, Strindberg wrote *himself.*

But that self changed radically over the years. At first he defined himself against Ibsen, convinced that this Norwegian "bluestocking" with his "Nora-cult" of feminism was spreading libels about his (Strindberg's) manhood. Ibsen responded: "I cannot write a line without that madman standing and staring down at me with his mad eyes."

It is true that throughout his life, Strindberg was subject to severe paranoid delusions. In the first masculine stage of his career, he represents himself as a brutal Naturalist often overcome (as in *The Father,*) by the superior wiles of the female sex and its belief in supernatural powers. But after a serious psychic breakdown in Paris when he believed witches were trying to electrocute him through the walls of his room, he began to identify himself with the female cause, putting women at the suffering center of such plays as *Easter*, *A Dream Play*, and *The Ghost Sonata*. When he learns to control his misogyny in later years, and soften his resistance to the female principle, he begins to face life with the quietism of a Buddhist saint, subordinating his defiant masculinity to the need for waiting, patience, and expiation.

But it is impossible to capture Strindberg in a defining moment that is not immediately contradicted by a radical change in style and attack. His plays are the psychic biography of a man who suffered greatly and made others suffer greatly, particularly his wives. His plays have the continuing power to provoke and offend, and sometimes even to heal.

Robert Brustein
Founding Director of the Yale and American Repertory Theatres
Distinguishing Scholar in Residence, Suffolk University
Senior Research Fellow, Harvard University

Strindberg

IN A MINUTE

AGE	DATE	
—	1849	**Enter Johan August Strindberg.**
5	1854	Heinrich Goebel invents the electric lightbulb.
13	1862	Bismarck becomes prime minister of Prussia.
14	1863	John Stuart Mill — *Utilitarianism*
16	1865	Abraham Lincoln assassinated at Ford's Theatre.
18	1867	Russia sells Alaska to the United States for $7.2 million.
19	1868	Johannes Brahms — *A German Requiem*
21	1870	Heinrich Schliemann begins the first modern excavation of Troy.
22	1871	Unification of Germany by Bismarck.
25	1874	First American zoo founded in Philadelphia.
28	1877	Henrik Ibsen — *The Pillars of Society*
30	**1879**	**August Strindberg — *The Red Room***
32	1881	Freedom of the press is established in France.
34	**1883**	**August Strindberg — *Lucky Peter's Journey***
36	1885	Mormons split into polygamous and monogamous sects.
37	1886	Friedrich Nietzsche — *Beyond Good and Evil*
39	**1888**	**August Strindberg — *Miss Julie***
43	1892	Rudolf Diesel patents the internal combustion engine.
44	1893	Art Nouveau defies conventions in Europe.
45	1894	George Bernard Shaw — *Arms and the Man*
46	1895	First U.S. pro football game played between two Pennsylvania towns.
48	1897	J. J. Thomson discovers the electron.
50	**1899**	**August Strindberg — *The Stronger***
52	1901	Ragtime jazz takes off in the red-light districts of New Orleans and St. Louis.
53	1902	Anton Chekhov — *The Three Sisters*
54	1903	Orville and Wilbur Wright successfully fly a powered plane.
56	1905	The 1814 union of Sweden and Norway dissolves.
58	**1907**	**August Strindberg — *A Dream Play***
61	1910	Tango is all the rage in the U.S. and Europe.
63	**1912**	**Exit August Strindberg.**

A snapshot of the playwright's world. From historical events to pop-culture and the literary landscape of the time, this brief list catalogues events that directly or indirectly impacted the playwright's writing. Play citations refer to premiere dates.

Strindberg

HIS WORKS

DRAMATIC WORKS

A Birthday Gift (lost)

The Freethinker

Hermione

In Rome

The Outlaw

Master Olof

Anno 48

The Secret of the Guild

Sir Bengt's Wife

Lucky Peter's Journey

The Robbers

The Father

Miss Julie

Creditors

The Stronger

Pariah

The People of Hemsö

Simoom

The Keys of Heaven

The First Warning

Debit and Credit

In the Face of Death

A Mother's Love

Playing with Fire

The Bond

This section presents a complete list of the playwright's works in chronological order. Titles appearing in another language indicate that they were first written and premiered in that language.

The Black Glove
The Great Highway

NOVELS

The Red Room
The People of Hemsö
By the Open Sea
The Gothic Rooms
Black Banners

FICTIONALIZED AUTOBIOGRAPHY

Journey into Detention
The Son of a Servant
Time of Ferment
In the Red Room
The Author
A Madman's Defense
The Inferno
The Monastery
Legends
Alone

SHORT NOVELS

Tschandala
The Roofing Ceremony
The Scapegoat

SHORT STORY COLLECTIONS

From Town and Gown
Swedish Destinies and Adventures
Married I
Actual Utopias
Married II

Men of the Skerries
Historical Miniatures

POETRY
Poems and Realities
Poems in Verse and Prose
Nights of Sleepwalking

ESSAYS AND OTHER
Vivisections
The Blue Books
Open Letters to the Intimate Theater
An Occult Diary

Onstage with Strindberg

Introducing Colleagues and
Contemporaries of August Strindberg

 THEATER

André Antoine, French director

Anton Chekhov, Russian playwright

Edward Gordon Craig, English stage designer

Gabriele D'Annunzio, Italian playwright

Henrik Ibsen, Norwegian playwright

Konstantin Stanislavsky, Russian director and actor

Oscar Wilde, Irish playwright

William Butler Yeats, Irish poet and playwright

 ARTS

Edgar Degas, French painter

Gustav Klimt, Austrian painter

Henri Matisse, French painter

Claude Monet, French painter

Edvard Munch, Norwegian painter

Pablo Picasso, Spanish painter

Giacomo Puccini, Italian composer

Auguste Rodin, French sculptor

 POLITICS/ MILITARY

Otto von Bismarck, German-Prussian statesman

Benjamin Disraeli, English prime minister

Alfred Dreyfus, French army officer

Victor Emmanuel II, Italian king

This section lists contemporaries whom the playwright may or may not have known.

Napoleon III, French ruler
King Oscar II, Swedish monarch
Theodore Roosevelt, American president
Queen Victoria, English monarch

SCIENCE

Marie Curie, French scientist
Charles Darwin, English naturalist
Albert Einstein, German-American physicist
Sigmund Freud, Austrian psychologist
Carl Jung, Swiss psychologist
Richard von Krafft-Ebing, German neurologist
Gregor Mendel, Austrian geneticist
Max Weber, German sociologist

LITERATURE

Joseph Conrad, English novelist
Fyodor Dostoevski, Russian novelist
Hermann Hesse, German novelist
James Joyce, Irish novelist
Franz Kafka, Austrian-Czech novelist
Guy de Maupassant, French writer
Herman Melville, American novelist
Emile Zola, French novelist

RELIGION/PHILOSOPHY

Henri Bergson, French philosopher
Benedetto Croce, Italian philosopher and critic
Ralph Waldo Emerson, American philosopher
William James, American philosopher
Karl Marx, German socialist philosopher
John Stuart Mill, English philosopher
Friedrich Nietzsche, German philosopher
Oswald Spengler, German philosopher

SPORTS

Charlotte Cooper, English tennis player

Dwight F. Davis, American tennis player

Isadora Duncan, American dancer

W. G. Grace, English cricketer

Thomas King, English boxer

Kid McCoy, American boxer

Marie Taglioni, Italian-Swedish ballerina

Cy Young, American baseball player

BUSINESS/INDUSTRY

Andrew Carnegie, Scots-American industrialist

William Durant, American founder of GM and Chevrolet

Henry Ford, American founder of the Ford Motor Company

King Camp Gillette, American businessman and inventor of the
safety razor

William Kellogg, American industrialist and founder of Kellogg

J. P. Morgan, American financier

John D. Rockefeller, American industrialist

Cornelius Vanderbilt, American entrepreneur

STRINGBERG

in an hour

FIRST THINGS FIRST

The Swedish playwright August Strindberg (1849–1912) remains, almost a century after his death, one of the most important Western playwrights on the world stage. Strindberg, a man of letters whose enormous output is staggering for its variety, played an essential role in the development of the modern theater.

EARLY LIFE

Strindberg was born on January 22, 1849, to Carl Oscar Strindberg, a shipping agent, and Eleonora Ulrica Norling, a former servant girl. He was one of eleven children, only seven of whom survived to adulthood. When Strindberg was four, his father declared bankruptcy, but eventually recovered financial security. His mother died of tuberculosis when he was thirteen; less than a year later, his father married the housekeeper.

As he records in his numerous autobiographical novels, such as *Son of a Servant*, his childhood was far from happy; he was a remote

---

This is the core of the book. The essay places the playwright in the context of his or her world and analyzes the influences and inspirations within that world.

and frequently withdrawn child. His education at the University of Uppsala was interrupted several times. At first he was to study medicine, but soon changed course to study the humanities, studying languages and literature. In 1871, he eventually passed his examinations in English, French, German, and Italian, as well as in modern literature. Through his early years, he also made several attempts at becoming an actor, but failed each time. Then, in 1869, he began writing plays, and in 1871 he was awarded a stipend by King Charles XV for his play *The Outlaw*.

A FAILURE AT MARRIAGE

As for marriage, he made three attempts, each time to a professional woman: Siri von Essen, a middling actress; Frida Uhl, an Austrian journalist; and Harriet Bosse, a highly talented Norwegian actress. In each relationship, however, he suffered mental and physical torment, largely due to his own mental problems and personal idiosyncrasies. These personal torments informed most of his work in the theater, as well as in such works as *The Red Room* (1879), a novel about bohemian café society, which was his first major breakthrough, and *Married* (1884), a collection of short stories. For the latter, he was prosecuted in Sweden on a charge of blasphemy but was acquitted.

SELF-EXILE AND SUCCESS ABROAD

Strindberg's relationship with Sweden was almost as turbulent as that with his wives. He had little success in his native country until fairly late in his life. Unhappy in his homeland, he abandoned Sweden and lived abroad in Switzerland, Germany, Austria, Denmark, and France. From 1889 onward, at least five major Strindberg plays were produced in Paris, several of them at Théâtre Libre. Among the plays performed were *The Father* and *Creditors*. But it was in Germany that his greatest success abroad was realized.

His "exile" had begun in 1882 and ended with his return to Sweden in 1896, and with that return, he began a series of some of his most famous and influential plays. It has been called his "Expressionist" period, although Expressionism as a visual art movement did not formally begin until 1905 in Germany, and in the German theater not until 1910. In retrospect, however, Strindberg's Expressionist plays were fully realized examples of that movement to come.

Strindberg's Expressionist experiments began as early as 1898 in *To Damascus*, and ended in 1909 with the pilgrimage play *The Great Highway*. Within those dates, he wrote two more parts of *To Damascus*, plus *A Dream Play* and *The Ghost Sonata*. He also wrote a sequence of more than twenty non-Expressionist historical plays based on Swedish history and written in the form of the chronicle play, the best examples of which are *Master Olof* (1872, first version), *Erik XIV* (1899), and *Gustav Adolf* (1903).

His plays of this period are profoundly experimental. In *A Dream Play*, space and time do not exist and memory is mixed with fantasy. It is of historical interest to note that Sigmund Freud, that other great experimenter with dreams, published *The Interpretation of Dreams* in Vienna in 1900, one year before Strindberg wrote *A Dream Play*.

WITH A LITTLE HELP FROM DARWIN

For all of the full-length plays he wrote, the one-act chamber play became a particular favorite with Strindberg. Chamber plays, whether in one or three acts, can be performed with a small cast in a small space with practically no props or costumes.

Strindberg believed that all full-length plays are written for the sake of a single, climatic scene, toward which everything preceding it leads. Why, then, he reasoned, should a playwright waste his or her energies on the complications of a full-length play when the climactic scene can be made independent and able to stand alone? This approach to theater was the result, to some extent, of his response to Darwin and the literary naturalists. Through the influence of Darwin and his theory of evolution, the literary naturalists saw life as a kind of trap, with all life-forms determined by heredity and the environment. Man was the helpless victim of that trap, namely of the past. Emile Zola, the French writer and a friend of Strindberg, is credited with starting the movement. He wrote the manifesto of naturalism in his 1880 essay "The Experimental Novel" (*Le Roman expérimental*).

Strindberg referred to this view as "little naturalism." He, however, adopted a view that he called "greater naturalism." Determinism was still a word in Strindberg's vocabulary, except that for him determinism was something that happened in the present, onstage and directly in front of the audience. For the literary naturalists, a character is what he is when the curtain rises because the environment has made him that way, and he acts accordingly, which is to say, consistently: His actions are predetermined by his past. For Strindberg, this approach was uninteresting; he wanted to see his characters modified within the environment of the here and now — on his stage. In a word, what Strindberg was after in his theater was *change*. He noted that *drama* in ancient Greek meant "occurrence," not action or conscious intrigue. He further noted that life does not fall into the neat patterns of constructed drama.

As critic Barry Jacobs notes, in *Strindberg's* Miss Julie: *A Play and Its Transpositions* "the conscious goals of [Strindberg's] characters are constantly being modified by the changing situation." Just like Sophocles' *Oedipus the King* and the other Greek tragedies, things are always in flux in Strindberg's plays. A character responds to an event happening, which immediately alters him or her. Then something else happens within the environment of the play, and that character is again modified. As the situation changes, so does the character, which brings us to the Strindbergian concept of the "characterless character." His characters, as Jacobs notes, are able to exercise free will. To create an effective one-act psychodrama, Strindberg had to destroy plot, and by doing so created a theater that still has much to teach us about drama.

MODERNISM AND THE NEW THEATER

Strindberg has been called "the playwright's playwright," perhaps because a vast stream of plays poured from him as if he were possessed, as if playwriting were his lifeline. Some of these plays are cornerstones in the history of Western theater; many are quite good. Perhaps more than half are of little importance, but none are less than artistically provocative. Along with Ibsen, Strindberg is one of the earliest voices of modernism in world drama; perhaps a better term is "modern consciousness" because of his psychological acuteness. He is the source of everything that is modern in drama. He anticipated the dilemma of modern man: Strindberg was one of the forerunners of the Theater of the Absurd. He was a fanatic experimenter who, as Sean O'Casey so insightfully declared, "shook down the living stars from heaven." Strindberg used his talents and passions to explore the "enigmas of the universe as well as those of dramatic form."

EARLY PLAYS AND THE FIRST SUCCESS

Strindberg wrote his first plays as a twenty-year-old in 1869: *The Freethinker* and *A Nameday Gift*. Michael Meyer, in *Strindberg: A Biography*, describes *The Freethinker* as containing "the usual beginner's faults; everyone holds forth at length, and none of the characters except the hero has any real life. But it shows that even this early Strindberg knew how to write dialogue." The following year he wrote two plays on historical themes, a format he would cultivate later in life. *Hermione* takes place in Classical Greece, and *In Rome* occurs around 1800. Both received encouraging praise from various sources. Then, in 1871, he wrote *The Outlaw*, a play set in twelfth-century Iceland about a chieftain's conversion to Christianity. But his use of the formal style of the Icelandic sagas clashed with his modern outlook and colloquial style. Later that year and into the next, he wrote what may be considered his first great play, *Master Olof*, a historical prose drama in five acts. He put the play through three major revisions, but ironically, it was the original version that was finally produced, in 1881. *Master Olof*, the story of a revolutionary young man intent on pulling down what is old in society but fearful of violence and a violent death, was the first play that Strindberg poured himself into. In an 1880 letter, Strindberg confided: "It is the story of my life."

But *Master Olof* was not well received because it was too modern for its time. Audiences expected a historical drama to be written in verse with characters delivering lengthy formal monologues. Instead, the play was written in prose and presented lifelike portraits rather than overblown historical figures. It required a style of acting that would not be used until later in the century, when Stanislavsky introduced method acting.

For the next four years Strindberg wrote no plays, though he had his first major breakthrough with the autobiographical novel *In the Red Room*. Other plays followed, though not terribly good ones. And yet, in the course of writing them, he hit on a subject that was not common for his time: modern marriage and the nature of sexual relations. This would become a major subject in his work, *The Father* being the first example.

NATURALISM AND THE FIRST MAJOR PLAYS

Strindberg's first major plays, *The Father* (1887), *Miss Julie* (1888), and *The Stranger* (1888–89), were written in the heyday of naturalism. This movement in the arts was stimulated by Darwin's *On the Origin of Species* and the historical and political observations of Marx in his *Critique of Political Economy*, both published in 1859. In addition to Zola, central figures in naturalism included the Goncourt brothers, Balzac, de Maupassant, and André Antoine, who founded Théâtre Libre in 1887, the influential experimental theater that first introduced Strindberg to Paris.

In *The Father*, Strindberg adopts the scientific approach advocated by Zola in his manifestoes. For Zola, the novelist is not just an observer or analyst, he or she is like a scientific experimenter. The novel, according to Zola in his essay "The Experimental Novel," constitutes the following: "to possess a knowledge of the mechanism of the phenomena inherent in man, to show the machinery of his intellectual and sensory manifestations, under the influences of heredity and environment, such as physiology shall give them to us, and then finally to exhibit man living in social conditions produced by himself, which he modifies daily, and in the heart of which he himself experiences a continual transformation."

For Strindberg, experimental writing meant bringing art close to actual life. He abandoned aesthetic distance or the conventional notion that the author is outside his or her work and must maintain a godlike detachment. As he says about his play *The Father*, he did not know if it was "something I have imagined or if my life was really like this." He raises the question of whether insight is something new that comes from experience, or whether it is something from within, a deep truth underneath experience that goes beyond common sense.

THE FATHER

As in so many of his plays and novels, Strindberg used his work as a means of exorcizing private demons. His decade-long disastrous marriage to Siri von Essen supplies the material for *The Father*.

The battle of the sexes is, however, not the only subject of the play; Strindberg was also obsessed with hypnotism and suggestion. He knew about the experiments of Hippolyte Bernheim, a French physician and neurologist who was a leading authority on hypnotism. Bernheim had studied how the power of suggestion can influence people who are awake. Strindberg had also studied Max Nordau's *Paradoxes*, which demonstrated how suggestion can affect normal, healthy minds. In

Strindberg's plays, the male is the more refined sex doomed to be crushed by the stronger, more primitive female, whose weapon is spiritual murder through suggestion. It is her will against his.

Men and Women: The Eternal Battle

The two principal characters in *The Father* are Adolph, also called the Captain, and his wife, Laura. The Captain is portrayed as weak of will, whereas his wife is strong willed. Laura is openly scornful of the Captain's inability to make a decision and stick with it.

The key power struggle between them concerns the upbringing and education of their daughter Bertha. Laura wants her to be raised at home under her supervision; the Captain wants her boarded out and educated in town. He believes Bertha needs to be free of her mother's excessive influence and that of the other women who live in the household so that she can be herself.

Woman, then, is the Captain's nemesis, as she is for many of Strindberg's males. How does the Captain fight a battle he knows he will inevitably lose? One possible and compelling choice is to not fight *because* he expects to lose in this battle over Bertha. For her part, Laura, as a member of the weaker sex dominated by men, is fighting for her very survival. The destruction of the male, of the Captain, is almost an incidental consequence of her struggle, as Morgan has it, "against her virtual annihilation as a human being," as Margery Morgan notes in *August Strindberg*. Morgan continues, "[w]ith an ambiguous touch, [Strindberg] makes the priest seem to endorse the triumph of Laura, the new order, at the end of the play, with an 'Amen!'"

Survival of the Fittest: Woman Triumphant

Laura has been actively against the Captain from the start. In her conversation with her brother, the Pastor, we learn that she did not marry the Captain for love but for security. Adolf was an officer in the cavalry (a socially prestigious position). He is educated, intellectually astute, a freethinker, even a scientist with impressive research papers to his credit: He was a good catch for her purposes.

Strindberg accepted the Darwinian proposition that the living struggle to survive and only the fittest prevail. And in Strindberg's lexicon, the fittest is the female, who will always have her way. She will win against all odds, including the male's greater physical strength, his schooled intelligence (largely denied women of the time), and his pride of place in a world that denigrates and discounts women.

Strindberg's Captain has one fatal flaw that makes him unable to fight for his survival. That flaw, as Strindberg makes clear in *The Father*, is his need for sex. From the beginning of their marriage, the Captain has turned a blind eye to Laura's efforts to dominate him, to deny him his traditional role as the dominant male, for one reason: sex. He has allowed himself to be systematically destroyed. He won't fight her, or at least, he won't fight to win. He merely puts up the pretence of a fight, if only to convince himself that he did his best. As Strindberg noted about this character (and about men in general):

> It is only in the presence of woman he is unmanly, and that is how she wants him, and the law of accommodation forces us to play the role our mistress requires. Yes, we sometimes have to play chaste, ingenuous, ignorant just to get the sexual intercourse we want!

The male, then, in Strindberg's eyes, is the prey of the female, whose one aim is to gain dominance in order to survive at the highest level within her grasp, a level at least higher than the one a patriarchal society has assigned her.

Laura has been ruthless in her struggle for control of their daughter. She has deliberately planted a poisonous seed of doubt in the Captain's mind, suggesting that he is not the child's father. This is a devastating blow to the Captain's pride. Furthermore, there is no way for him to prove his paternity; only one person knows for certain — the mother. The possibility that Bertha is not his child also denies him his immortality, which is even more devastating to him than loss of pride. As he says to Laura in the play, "Since I don't believe in an afterlife, the child has become that for me, my conception of immortality, the only immortality than has any basis in reality. Take that from me, and you cut short my life."

But she does take it from him. Knowing that this has devastated him, Laura moves in, literally, for the kill. She leads the Captain step-by-step into insanity and, most likely, death by stroke. Strindberg makes the criminality of Laura's methods clear in the third-act discussion between Laura and her brother, the Pastor. The Pastor is all too aware of what she has done to the Captain, driving him to insanity. He calls her crime "[a] little innocent murder that the law can't get at; an unconscious crime" and a "remarkable invention." Every bit as remarkable is the Captain's twenty-year ability to be unconscious of his subservience to Laura in return for the desired reward — sex.

Casting the Play

In a letter dated October 17, 1887, the year of the play's composition, Strindberg, recognizing the larger-than-life-size characters of his two principals, wondered who would ultimately play the Captain and Laura. He knew that the play could easily be destroyed by a miscast actor, even made to seem ridiculous. For the Captain, his advice was to cast an actor "with a generally healthy temperament." Ideally he should possess the "superior, self-ironic, lightly skeptical tone of a man of the world," a man who "conscious of his advantage, goes to meet his fate in a relatively carefree mood, wrapping himself in death in the spider's web he cannot tear to shreds because of natural laws . . . To me he represents especially here a manliness people have tried to disparage, taken away from us and awarded to the third sex [i.e. feminists]!"

As for Laura, she should not be played as a virago; that way lies melodrama. She is a woman of her time, who, like many of Ibsen's women, is determined to get the upper hand in a male world. A product of mid-nineteenth-century society, she has decided that enough is enough, but she has, in the process, lost sight of just whom she married. Neither side in this equation is free of blame.

MISS JULIE

With a mind as diverse and conflicted as Strindberg's, it should not be surprising that his viewpoint changes from play to play. If in *The Father*, the female is the victor in the struggle for survival, in *Miss Julie*, written within the next year, it is Jean, the servant struggling to rise, who wins. The ascendance of Jean is consistent with another of Strindberg's social perceptions — that the aristocratic class was a degenerate bunch of hangers-on. In nineteenth-century Sweden, the aristocracy was steadily losing ground. The 1860s, for example, saw the House of Lords abolished in the Swedish parliament, an act that promised eventual control by the slowly rising lower classes. Strindberg likely identified with Jean, for he, like Jean, had to struggle for position; he even referred to himself in the title of one of his novels as the son of a servant. To him, Jean was, as one critic has put it, "the coming gentleman by virtue of his energy and ability" — even though Jean is not a particularly attractive character from a moral standpoint.

A Slice of Life? Not Quite

Strindberg called *Miss Julie* the first naturalistic play in Scandinavia. Naturalist theater and literature rejected the artful selection and arrangement of events. Life is chaos, insisted the naturalists, and therefore the chaos of life must be at the center of art. Art, in the scientific age, must be as objective as a scientific experiment; it must grow out of a scientific study of a small section of life itself (like the study of a culture on the slide of a microscope). The whole movement was a reaction to the excesses of romanticism.

But *Miss Julie* falls short of the naturalist program because it fails to present a "slice of life," a central tenet of the movement. In his own defense, in the preface to *Miss Julie*, Strindberg describes what he has done in contradiction to certain aspects of Zola's manifesto:

> Since my characters are modern . . . I have shown them to be split and vacillating, a fusion of old and new. . . . My souls (or characters) are agglomerations of cultures past and present, bits and pieces gathered from books and newspapers, scraps of humanity, torn tatters of once splendid clothing that has fallen to rags, just as a human soul is patched together. . . . I have eschewed the symmetrical, mathematically constructed dialogue of the sort in favor with the French, and have given their minds free reign to operate irregularly, as happens in real life.

No question, then, that Strindberg had read and digested his Zola (they were, after all, friends), but he was too much the artist to completely abandon aesthetic selection and order. He selected and arranged and as a result achieved one of the most durable and brilliantly constructed pieces of theater. Walter Johnson, in *Strindberg and the Historical Drama*, sums up the Strindberg achievement.

> Strindberg did consider [*Miss*] *Julie* naturalistic, and, granting the qualifications of selection and arrangement, one will have to admit that Strindberg within those limits has given us an artist's presentation of an inner recreation of a segment of life. The one-act form; a theme that is universal and timeless; a plot that was partly taken right out of life and could have been almost completely; a dialogue that strikes one as natural conversation, in terms of the situation, the particular people, the time, and the place; the decidedly realistic setting and staging; and the characterization—all these are in keeping with what Strindberg believed was naturalistic, always, it must be remembered, as seen and heard through Strindberg's eyes and ears and transformed in the creative process.

A Matter of Heredity

In *Miss Julie* both ends of the social spectrum meet, an aristocratic young woman of twenty-five and the healthy, ruggedly handsome, sexually provocative, and ambitious young servant five years her senior. It is midsummer eve, June 24, just past the summer solstice, when the days never seem to end in Scandinavia. The body and mind tire but cannot rest, because of the powerful influence of the sun. Life is a constant buzz, ears ring, blood surges, the mind is not in control — all of which the feast day celebration of St. John the Baptist happily exaggerates. In the course of the play, Miss Julie is seduced by Jean and as a consequence, unable to face her disgrace, commits suicide.

The time of the play is one of many factors used by Strindberg to lead to the final tragedy. Another is that Miss Julie is having her menstrual period. Also important are the recent breakup of Miss Julie's engagement to a young lawyer and her mixed and confusing parentage. Her mother, who is lower class and has radically feminist attitudes, has raised her daughter to despise the male sex and to exalt the female as superior. Conversely, her aristocratic and traditional father has taught her to view her own sex as despicable.

Parallel Action: A Guide to Meaning

One theatrical device that Strindberg uses in his plays to good effect is *parallel action*, and *Miss Julie* has two that are of particular brilliance. The first appears early on. Diana, Miss Julie's female dog, has recently escaped her closely protected environment and run off with the gamekeeper's mongrel mutt. Diana is an aristocratic pure-bred dog with a pedigree never meant to mix with riff-raff like the gamekeeper's mutt. She has been carefully protected from doing so, as has Miss Julie. The dog's name, Diana, is after the Roman virgin goddess of chastity and the hunt. At the play's beginning, Miss Julie is herself a virgin, as her constrained and restrictive upbringing has insisted.

But Diana does escape, indulging her natural appetite for the first time, just as Miss Julie will do with her servant Jean later in the play. Diana is now pregnant, a situation that, we learn, Miss Julie does not want to deal with. At first Miss Julie insists that Diana be shot for her indiscretion, but she finally decides to attempt an abortion and has the cook prepare a concoction to induce a miscarriage. Miss Julie's solution for herself will be more severe.

The second parallel action concerns Serena, Miss Julie's female finch. The tiny bird is pampered, held captive in a cage, and is expected to sing for her captor. Miss Julie, too, is a captive, not in a cage but in a class no less restrictive. One critic has suggested that the finch's name, Serena, implies "the serenity of the artificially protected captive to sing appropriately for the pleasure of her human keepers." Just as the finch has its head cut off on the chopping-block by a meat cleaver wielded by Jean, Miss Julie will slice her own throat with the razor that Jean will put in her hand. Possibly the finch's blood spilled by the brutal Jean is, in addition to foreshadowing Miss Julie's eventual suicide, also the sexual blood not only of menstruation (as has been noted by others) but the blood of her first sexual experience at the hands of a human mutt.

Zero Plus Zero Equals Zero

Miss Julie's suicide at the play's end is motivated by many things, but one in particular stands out. Like her protected Diana, Miss Julie has fallen from her height and everybody knows it, in particular the servant revelers who enter the empty kitchen and sing a lascivious song while she and Jean are at it in his room. There is no place she can hide and no way she can reassert her former status. Scandal is her nemesis just as surely as it is the nemesis of Ibsen's Hedda Gabler. Hedda is unquestionably pregnant and hates herself for that weakness because it identifies her as female, a fact of herself that she, too, was taught to despise by her father, General Gabler, who raised her as a boy. Miss

Julie may well fear herself pregnant by Jean, and we have seen how she handled the feared pregnancy of her Diana, whose status would have been compromised, therefore making death a preferable choice.

To sum it up, Miss Julie has violated everything she was raised to be. She has betrayed her mother's feminism and her father's patriarchal worldview, the two self-contradictory realities of her being. She is nothing less than no one. In her great, passionate confession to Jean toward the play's conclusion, she finally is able to say: "I don't even have a *self* I can call my own." The two warring sides of her imposed nature cancel each other out and leave her nothing less than nothing.

The Power of Will

If Strindberg made central use of the power of will, or suggestion, in *The Father*, he makes even more theatrical use of it in *Miss Julie*. The play ends with a horrific scene in which all means of escape seem closed to Miss Julie, except for one: suicide. She knows she must do it, but she hasn't the willpower and asks Jean to supply what she lacks. During this last scene, the body of her finch brutally slaughtered by Jean is still visible on the bloody chopping block.

CREDITORS
Writing Too Close to Home

Strindberg wrote *Creditors* in August/September 1888 very soon after *Miss Julie*. On September 29, he wrote the following to the Swedish publisher Joseph Seligmann:

> The attached tragedy was written for the Théâtre Libre at the same time as *Miss Julie*. I didn't want to publish it in Swedish because my enemies always write commentaries on my work designed to damage me. But now that I have seen from the attached advertisement how intimately one is allowed to write, I send for your perusal this play, which is

finer than *Miss Julie* and in which I have more successfully achieved this new form [the one-act play], in the hope that you may be willing to print it with the other play [*Miss Julie*] in one volume. The plot is exciting, as spiritual murder must be; the analysis and the motivation are exhaustive, the viewpoint impartial; the author judges no one, he merely explains and forgives; and although he has made even the promiscuous woman sympathetic, this does not mean that he is advocating promiscuity. On the contrary, he says specifically that it is a bad thing, because of the disagreeable consequences which it brings.

Seligmann refused the play not because he found it immoral, but because it was too intimate and too transparently based on Strindberg's own marriage to Siri von Essen.

The autobiographical nature of the play is unquestioningly at times painful. Strindberg, himself, feared that Baron Gustav Wrangel, von Essen's former husband, would reappear and steal her back and even take revenge for his portrayal in the play as the husband of Tekla. Strindberg's self-portrait is the character of Adolf, who, through the power of "suggestion," is ultimately destroyed by his two adversaries, his wife, Tekla, and her former husband, Gustav.

Psychic Murder: The Sex Wars

Creditors is a model of dramatic economy, everything reduced to the absolute minimum, even to following the classical unities of time, place, and action. This three-character play is divided into three duologues in a single act. It is the epitome of what Strindberg described as the one-act genre: a play reduced to its climactic scene.

The first of the duologues takes place between Gustav, Tekla's first husband, and Adolf, her second and current husband, who does not know who Gustav is, never having met him. The second is between

Tekla and Adolf, with Gustav listening in from a neighboring room. The third is between Tekla and Gustav, with Adolf listening in.

As to their types, Gustav is Strindberg's prime example of the superior man. A professional educator, proud of his superior intellect, he is, in Nietzschean terms, the Superman. Adolf, on the other hand, is an artist whose sensitivity is equal to Gustav's intellect. And Tekla is the attractive woman that neither of the two men can manage to free themselves from. Gustav, as the intellectual, deals with people by analyzing, probing, and dissecting. He forces Adolf to analyze his life — his art, ideals, wife, marriage. He is out for revenge, driven in part by his hurt pride and loss of honor. Adolph, on the other hand, is the artist who feels and senses rather than analyzes. He is a moral idealist and emotionally and mentally vulnerable. Tekla enjoys sex without guilt and takes advantage of people and opportunities without being aware of what she is doing or of the effect she is having. Her role in Adolph's murder is unintentional and unconscious.

In the play, Gustav calls Tekla a cannibal, a serpent, a thief, a little devil, and a monster. Gustav's description of her is clearly derived from Strindberg's narrative essay "Psychic Murder," which he wrote on Ibsen's play *Rosmersholm*. In the essay, Strindberg speaks of Rebekka West as having driven Rosmer's wife, Beata, to her death by means of suggestion and calls her "an unconscious cannibal, who has devoured the dead wife's soul." In Strindberg's play, we see the effect of Tekla's machinations on Adolph, how she has depleted or cannibalized him, and we also observe Gustav at work, as he further depletes Adolf's reserve for survival. Gustav is clearly out for revenge in one of Strindberg's most masterful scenes.

The summary of Strindberg's essay "Psychic Murder" will make clear the strategy employed above, as well as in many another of Strindberg's best plays.

Now one creates a majority against him, puts him in the wrong, exposes his ideas, attributes ideas to him other than his own, robs him of his means of existence, denies him social standing, makes him ridiculous — in a word, tortures and lies him to death or makes him go crazy instead of killing him. The expressions "tortured to death," "driven him crazy," "kill him with silence," "boycott," "utterly ruin" more and more become everyday terms, and the little innocent words conceal or reveal just as many major crimes as the dungeons in feudal castles.

Sucking Lifeblood

That same winter, as Strindberg was planning a Scandinavian experimental theater based on Antoine's Théâtre Libre, he conceived of *Creditors* as one of that theater's first works, and, not unsurprising for Strindberg, he offered the "vampire" role of Tekla to von Essen. She accepted the part, but as it happened, she never played it.

When the play was finally produced, in Copenhagen on March 9, 1889, it was performed miserably by an inexperienced actress playing Tekla and an incompetent young actor playing Adolph who was so frightened by the role and by the experience of being onstage that he scarcely spoke. Only Gustav was well represented. And to that actor Strindberg gave a specific guide to the playing of the part:

> For God's sake, act it throughout with a playful *bonhomie*, like a man who knows he is superior. And above all the scene when Gustav tells how his divorce took place, merely as an experiment in psychological destruction — so that Tekla speaks the truth when she says of Gustav that he doesn't "preach or moralize." . . . In a word: Gustav must be like a cat playing with a mouse before he sinks his teeth into it. Never malignant, never moralizing, never preaching!

In *Creditors*, we see two of Strindberg's archetypal characters: the Strindbergian superior (Gustav) and the Strindbergian inferior (Tekla). Tekla feeds off Adolf, sucking his lifeblood by draining him of words and ideas; it is the only means she has to exist as a human being. She is the vampire. It is by that means that she has the "strength" to wear him down until he finally expires. Tekla acts unconsciously, as a parasite. Her parasitic draining of Adolph's words, ideas, and volition has weakened him and made him an easy prey for the undermining superiority of Gustav's intelligence.

Creditors, as one early critic put it, though a pretty terrible play is terribly good. It is one of Strindberg's most powerful and stage-worthy plays.

THE STRONGER

The Stronger, a one-act play — a sketch, really, since it occupies only half a dozen pages at best — is universally considered the quintessential short play and a superb monologue of great psychological profundity. Written by Strindberg in 1888–89 for his proposed Experimental Theater repertory, it was intended for his first wife, Siri von Essen, in the role of Mrs. X.

In this triangle, two actresses, one married, Mrs. X, and one unmarried, Miss Y, meet accidentally at a café while Christmas shopping and review their past rivalry in love for Mrs. X's husband. The subject of the discussion, the husband, never appears, and only one of the women, Mrs. X, speaks, while the other, Miss Y, merely reacts. To say "merely" is, however, to minimize the silent role, for it presents challenges every bit as great as the role of Mrs. X.

In *The Stronger*, Strindberg demonstrates his keen insight and capacity for observing human nature. The underlying question of the play is which of the two women is the stronger: the married actress, who takes all in stride, bends with the winds, and survives in the dog-eat-dog world or the silent Miss Y, who, as Mrs. X says, has failed to bend and has broken like a dry reed.

But is Mrs. X's observation correct or is it wishful thinking? Near the end of the play, she observes that Miss Y, rather than going after her prey aggressively, merely sits like a cat at the rat hole and outwaits it. At the end of her monologue, she catalogues all that Miss Y lacks and has lost and all that she, Mrs. X, has. Miss Y, she notes, can neither love nor hate. Mrs. X has a home and a baby; Miss Y has neither. According to Mrs. X, everything Miss Y puts her hand to becomes worthless and sterile. Her silence, furthermore, indicates stupidity not strength: She doesn't have a thought in her pretty little head. And yet, that quiet, nearly predatory silence may unnerve Mrs. X more than she's willing to acknowledge. The answer to which is the stronger can be found, perhaps, in Strindberg's "Psychic Murder" essay quoted above: "[K]ill him with silence." Mrs. X may in fact be announcing her own eventual loss of her husband to Miss Y — except that she is currently so secure in her marriage and family that she is unaware of her unconscious premonition.

PLAYING WITH FIRE

When Strindberg began writing *Playing with Fire* in 1892, he had just been through a series of highly stressful situations. He had returned to Sweden in 1889 for the first time in six years, having suffered deeply from the rapid collapse of his experimental theater in Copenhagen. He was all but penniless, creditors hounded him — loans from his brother and his publisher kept him going — and his marriage to Siri von Essen was in name only. Finally, in March 1891, his marriage was granted a year's separation pending a final dissolution.

In the planning stage was another experimental theater to be established in a restaurant dining room in a district just north of Stockholm where he was living during the year's separation. In spring 1892, in anticipation of the new theater, he wrote four one-act plays: *The First Warning, Debit and Credit, The Face of Death,* and *Mother Love.*

A few weeks later, he wrote the long one-act *Playing with Fire,* one of only three comedies in Strindberg's otherwise very serious career. But though a comedy, *Playing with Fire* has, nonetheless, a decidedly bitter taste. He wrote it as his spiteful revenge for an unfortunate slight that he had suffered from a friend the summer before. The play is also based on Strindberg's visit to Baron Wrangel's home a decade earlier. At the time, the baron was in love with his cousin and was willing to let his wife, Siri von Essen, have an affair with Strindberg. The affair ended in von Essen's divorce from the baron and her marriage to Strindberg — the same marriage that was now on the rocks.

Caught in the Nets of One's Own Weaving

Playing with Fire is not easy to perform. It can too easily be mistaken for farce, despite the fact that its basis is very serious. The atmosphere is one of Chekhovian boredom and wasted lives. Its characters are caught in a permanent stasis, a situation that they refuse to change because they are not aware of it, or, perhaps, because they *choose* not to be aware of it. They live out their upper-middle-class lives as comfortably as possible on the way to their eventual demise. As one character says: "We've woven our own nets and now we're caught in them." A fairly perceptive statement for these people to make, but it leads nowhere but back to square one.

Strindberg's biographer Michael Meyer is quite correct when he notes that the play requires a "claustrophobic atmosphere of heat, boredom and sensuality . . . The set should be a sun-trap, with bright light beating in through the glass and every window closed; it must not be airy." It is a play in which every character but one lusts after a sexual partner that is other than his or her own. Knut, the son, and his wife, Kerstin, have spent the night making noisy love, overheard by their visitor, Axel. But their lovemaking is merely to pass the time; there is no affection between them, let alone love. Kerstin is infatuated with Axel, and Axel with Kerstin. The Father is intent on making time with Adèle, a family relative, and Adèle is intent on Axel.

Meyer is right again when he notes that the scenes between Kerstin and Axel "call for black comedy of a very high order." They are clever operators, both of them, and they play cat and mouse games with each other, switching roles from time to time. "Cat and mouse, and I'm the mouse! And I'm caught in your trap!" observes Kerstin of Axel during one of their encounters. Their capacity for deception operates not merely on others, but on themselves as well. Perhaps it makes life a bit more interesting for them than it actually is. The cliché of the title, which refers to illicit or ill-advised sex, is brought up by the Mother. "You know," she says, "what they say about playing with fire." And her son Knut responds: "I know, I know, but I'm too old to start learning. Besides, look at me! Do I look like I need to worry?" For that misplaced self-confidence, one might say, he will pay in the end, and he does when his father hands back to him the wife who, just minutes before, he admitted he could very easily get along without. *Playing with Fire* is a brittle, sophisticated comedy that has had considerable success in the world's theaters.

THE DANCE OF DEATH
Part I: A Marriage Made in Hell

The Dance of Death, Part I has been performed internationally more than any other Strindberg play. It is constantly revived in the professional theater and has drawn some of the world's greatest actors. It has also served as one of the modern theater's most influential plays, having spawned such works as Albee's *Who's Afraid of Virginia Woolf?*, Anouilh's *Waltz of the Toreadors*, and possibly even Beckett's *Endgame*, as well as some of the plays of Ionesco.

The play dissects a hellish marriage. Its location is in a round, gray-stone fortress on an island off the coast of Sweden, named, appropriately, Little Hell. In it live the Captain, an elderly military officer, and his middle-aged wife, Alice, a once-promising actress. They are approaching their twenty-fifth wedding anniversary with nothing to celebrate but their life of corrosive isolation, frustration, boredom, and mutual hatred. In the play, Strindberg suggests that

Edgar and Alice had at one time great potential for personal and social good. But the two are inherently selfish and egotistical and refuse to take any responsibility for themselves or the state of their marriage; they are experts at rationalization. The only bond in their otherwise hateful union is sexual attraction.

So evil is the atmosphere of this marriage that Alice's cousin Kurt, who appears unexpectedly, having been assigned to the island as quarantine master, remarks: "But tell me, what are you up to in this house? What happens? The walls smell like poison. I felt sick the moment I walked in. I wouldn't be staying if I hadn't promised Alice. There are corpses hoarded under the floorboards. Such hatred here it makes it hard to breathe." In the course of the evening, the Captain suffers two heart attacks, which are approvingly applauded by Alice. Kurt finds the rampant fury in the household too much to bear and leaves, allowing for a grotesque and darkly comedic reconciliation between the Captain and Alice.

Part II: Vampiric Vendettas and Other Assorted Designs

The Dance of Death, Part II was an attempt by Strindberg to lighten the negative mood that disturbed contemporary critics at the early performances of Part I. It takes place during the summer following Part I in an oval living room decorated in white and gold, a far cry from the gray-stone fortress of Part I. But Strindberg only partially succeeded in lightening the mood.

The Captain carries out a bitter vendetta against Kurt. Allan, Kurt's son, is in love with the Captain's daughter, Judith, but Judith torments him by flirting with other men. The Captain wants to marry Judith to the old Colonel. To get Allan out of the way, he has him transferred to a remote military post in Lapland. The Captain is also maneuvering for Kurt to lose his house. Judith, in opposition to the Captain finally, reciprocates Allan's love, swearing she will follow him to the ends of the earth. She also sends an insolent telegram to the old Colonel. The Captain, upon learning how plans have failed, has a final stroke and dies. Alice initially triumphs over his death, but then at the end realizes that, for all her hatred of him, she once truly loved him.

Mood Swings and Creativity

It is fair to say that there are few plays in the modern theater that are more bleak than *The Dance of Death*, Part I. Strindberg wrote another play, *Easter*, simultaneously with *Dance of Death*, Part I. *Easter*, by contrast, is a play of reconciliation and hope, sharply at odds with its pessimistic and hate-filled partner. "But," says Meyer, "that he should have written the two plays practically simultaneously is not as incongruous as some critics have supposed. It was a part of Strindberg's paranoid-schizophrenic character that he alternated with bewildering rapidity between opposing moods. Taken together, the two plays portray him more accurately and fully than either work considered by itself."

As was usual with Strindberg's plays, first productions of *The Dance of Death* were abroad. *Dance of Death*, Part I premiered in Cologne; a few months later, both parts were performed in Berlin. *Dance of Death*, Part I was not performed in Sweden until 1905, five years after its completion, and drew a mixed press. One critic described it as "a pathological study of various physical and spiritual illnesses: erotic hysteria and sclerosis of the heart and the like. A hospital theatre would be the most appropriate locale for *The Dance of Death*." This critic, however, was in the minority. The play was a great success, with eighty-five performances. Part II followed two months later and won even higher praise, principally because it softened to some degree the hatred and pessimism of Part I and permitted a hopeful resolution. Part I, however, has always been one of Strindberg's greatest successes worldwide.

Strindberg was not reticent about advising actors regarding how to play his roles. August Falck, the prime mover in the establishment of the Intimate Theater in 1907, writes in his 1935 memoir, *Five Years with Strindberg*, of the playwright advising his actor-director:

> "*The Dance of Death*, my boy! That's my best play!" Strindberg often repeated . . . "The Captain! What a part!" And he jumped up and acted it for me. "A refined demon! Evil shines out of his eyes, which sometimes flash with a glint of satanic humor. His face is bloated with liquor and corruption, and he so relishes saying evil things that he almost sucks them, tastes them, rolls them round his tongue before spitting them out. He thinks of course that he is cunning and superior, but like all stupid people he becomes at such moments a pitiful and petulant wretch." And with sweet-sour, fawning expressions, with gestures both jaunty and pitiful, he walked around or threw himself down into a chair. What he particularly often liked to act was the powerful scene when Alice, with a bored expression, plays the march *The Dance of the Boyars*, which incites and hypnotizes the Captain to dance—wildly and clumsily, terrifyingly. At such moments he was an excellent actor—a great dramatic talent. His vivid impersonation remains for ever in my mind's eye and echoes in my ear.

The *Dance of Death* is without question a central text in the history of the modern theater. In almost every respect, it gave form to the modern manner of playwriting. Strindberg's jagged, uneven dramas, with his moody, sometimes violently emotional characters, has been the model for many younger playwrights.

A NEW THEATER FOR NEW FORMS

Between 1898 and 1903 Strindberg experienced his most creative period, during which he wrote more than twenty plays, including some of his greatest. His mind was in turmoil both personally and creatively. He was suffering through his third and most volatile marriage and perhaps needed to find a new form of theater capable of fully expressing the deep despair he was feeling.

In his need for a new form of theater, and of art in general, he was not alone. The turn of the century saw many artists and thinkers restlessly seeking and developing new forms of thought and expression. In 1897, the painter Gustav Klimt founded the Secessionist group of artists — painters, musicians, sculptors — in Vienna, a breakaway group determined to represent reality not just realistically but it in exciting, unexpected, and decorative ways. These artists wanted to get to the bottom of things rather than be stuck on the surface. The Cubists and abstract painters overthrew the maxim that artists should represent recognizable objects in a recognizable setting, whether temporal or spatial. In 1896, Chekhov, in *The Seagull*, has his Treplev, an unpublished and unperformed young playwright, denounce the traditional theater and cry out for "new forms."

This rumble shook the art world at the end of the nineteenth century, and Strindberg was a part of it, as his preface to *A Dream Play* makes very clear.

> Anything can happen, everything is possible and probable. Space and time do not exist. Based on a slight foundation of reality, imagination wanders afield and weaves new patterns comprised of mixtures of recollections, experiences, unconstrained fantasies, absurdities, and improvisations. Characters split, double, and multiply; they evaporate, crystallize, dissolve, and reconverge. But one single consciousness governs them all — that of the dreamer. For him there are no secrets, no incongruities, no scruples, and no laws. He neither condemns nor does he acquit — he merely reports. And since there is generally more pain than pleasure in the dream, a tone of melancholy and sympathy for all things runs through the swaying narrative. Sleep, the liberator, is often tortuous; and yet when pain is at its worst, the sufferer is wakened and reconciled with reality. For however agonizing reality may

be, it is, at this moment, when compared with the torments
of the dream, a joy.

A DREAM PLAY

A Dream Play is one of the most influential plays of the modern
theater in that it led directly to Expressionism, Dadaism, Symbolism,
Surrealism, and the Theater of the Absurd. The thrust of the play is to
discover the reason for humankind's misery. The Indian god Indra
sends his daughter to earth to find the answer. In her wanderings, she
takes on many roles so that she can experience human misery
firsthand, the worst and most devastating of which is the state of
marriage (a reflection of Strindberg's tormented marriage to his third
wife, Harriet Bosse). The play is filled with esoteric symbolic elements,
such as the Growing Castle, which at the end burns as though in a
purging fire. The daughter enters the Growing Castle, now burning,
and sees a wall of faces that are questioning and mourning. While the
castle burns, a flower bud on the roof bursts open into a giant
chrysanthemum. When the daughter returns to Indra, she tells him
what she has so painfully learned, that man is to be pitied. The play is
an expression of modern pessimism. It is a recognition of how limited
human beings are, trapped by the demands of their egos, and how
there is little hope for improvement in a community made up of
individuals struggling for survival and personal advantage.

Strindberg called *A Dream Play* "My most blessed drama, the
child of my greatest suffering." So revolutionary was it that it is only in
the last few decades that the theater has developed enough to be able
to stage its visual effects well.

A THEATER OF ONE'S OWN

In 1907, the Intimate Theater in Stockholm was founded, a
collaboration between Strindberg and August Falck. The theater

seated only 161 people and was so small and close that the slightest gesture, the flick of an eyelash, could be perceived and understood. The theater was inspired by Max Reinhardt's Kammerspiele (Chamber Theater) in Berlin and the Théâtre Libre in Paris, as well as Stanislavsky's Moscow Arts Theater and the Abbey Theatre in Dublin.

The five plays written for the Intimate Theater's first season were *Storm*, *The Ghost Sonata*, *The Burned House*, *The Pelican*, and *The Black Glove*. Having been written within a short period of time, they naturally share a great deal in common in regard to images and themes. Among the related motifs are the consuming fire, the child lost and found, the return of the past in the present, and the vampire (or evil mother) who instead of nourishing strength drains it.

STORM

Storm, written in January/February 1907, is an excellent example of what Strindberg meant when he spoke of the chamber play as a genre. Plot is nonexistent. Characterization is minimal and left to suggestion. It is an ensemble piece with no star roles. Every one of the characters is central to the piece and contributes to the main theme of human loneliness. Last but not least, atmosphere and mood are preeminent. In *Storm*, life is in a holding pattern. There is a silence so profound that it can be heard. The people in this apartment house live apart, in isolation from their neighbors, whom they don't even know and aren't curious to know. Time seems stopped, and life hangs in abeyance. Strindberg, in fact, toyed with calling it *The Silent House*. And it is no accident that the play is set at twilight, neither day nor night but somewhere in between. As for the play's mood, it cannot be captured in even a medium-sized theater; it needs an intimate space. Strindberg had finally achieved what he most wanted — the seamless joining of play and playing space.

Strindberg chose as *Storm*'s theme his marriage with his third wife (parted now for five years), Harriet Bosse. He would see her occasionally when she was in Stockholm. He kept in touch and generally felt close to her. She, however, had fallen in love with an actor whom she was soon to marry, and Strindberg was troubled by the same thought that had tormented him when his marriage with Siri von Essen ended, namely that his daughter would transfer her love from him to a stepfather. As Meyer notes, *Storm* was a kind of warning to Bosse, much the same as *Creditors* had served as a warning to von Essen. He wrote to Bosse shortly after the play had been completed that it had been "a painful poem, with which to write you and our child out of my heart." *Storm* is a highly personal play. Meyer notes the circumstances under which Strindberg wrote the play:

> The previous summer he had spent alone in their flat in Östermalm, the fashionable quarter of Stockholm. Then, as now, most of the inhabitants left town during the warm season, but in those days their places were not taken by tourists, and the city seemed deserted. He saw hardly anyone except his brother Axel, who used to come and play Beethoven to him on the piano. On the mantelpiece he kept a large photograph of Harriet, with candles on either side. On 17 July he noted that the previous evening the street lamps had been lit for the first time that summer (at one time he planned to entitle the play *The First Lamp*). A few weeks later, he wrote: "Today, 2 August, ideal weather at last. Thunder and rain. One can breathe."

The description here is precisely the description given in the opening stage direction of *Storm*, even to the picture on the mantelpiece with candles on either side, and the play's theme is indeed the expulsion from the heart of the Gentleman's former wife and daughter.

THE GHOST SONATA
Appearance versus Reality

The principal theme of *The Ghost Sonata* is how appearances can deceive and disguise reality, a theme that occupied the minds of many playwrights at the turn of the century, most notably the Viennese Arthur Schnitzler and the Sicilian Luigi Pirandello. Michael Meyer quotes Strindberg in 1905 as writing:

> Life is so horribly ugly, we human beings so utterly evil, that if a writer were to portray everything he saw and heard no one could bear to read it. There are things which I remember having seen and heard in good, respectable and well-liked people, but which I have blotted out from my mind because I could not bring myself to speak of them and do not wish to remember them. Breeding and education are only masks to hide our bestiality, and virtue is a sham. The best we can hope for is to conceal our wretchedness. Life is so cynical that only a swine can be happy in it; and any man who sees beauty in life's ugliness is a swine! Life is a punishment. A hell. For some a purgatory, for none a paradise. We are compelled to commit evil and to torment our fellow mortals.

It is a statement written midway between *A Dream Play* and *The Ghost Sonata* and in a very profound way unites them thematically.

One cannot watch a performance of *The Ghost Sonata* without shifting in one's seat in discomfort over the bleakness and cruelty of the action onstage. In a letter to his German translator, Strindberg wrote that the play is as horrible as life itself when we tear away the veils from our eyes and face reality. He saw the corruption of life presented in *The Ghost Sonata* as symptomatic of life in general, except that we are too proud to admit it.

Strindberg's characters in the play are based on real people he saw, sometimes daily, on his walks in the upscale Stockholm suburb of Östermalm. Unlike Strindberg's other plays, which take place in homes like his own, *The Ghost Sonata* emerged from what he had heard and observed and also what he guessed at about the homes of his neighbors.

Stripping Away Defenses

In addition to the discrepancy between appearance and reality, there are at least two additional themes of *The Ghost Sonata*: idealism, represented by the young student Arkenholz, and the vampirism of Hummel, the man in the wheelchair. There is some evil force in every life, Strindberg maintains, that eats at the very core of our being, that sucks our energy and destroys our will — and will is a major element in *The Ghost Sonata*. Hummel's willpower enables him to possess the idealistic young Arkenholz. Like in *The Father*, will here is a powerful and evil force.

The Ghost Sonata is a dream play, a form that allowed Strindberg to strip away the defenses we generally use to protect ourselves — the masks, the personas we assume to make life an easier, less deadly burden. In many Strindberg plays, life and people are closely analyzed. In *The Ghost Sonata*, analysis is taken over by intuition, rationality is usurped by insight. Knowledge comes suddenly, as a revelation.

Like *A Dream Play*, *The Ghost Sonata* is a play of despair over the misery of the human condition. Arkenholz in the play's final sentences, through his lament over the dead Daughter, grieves over the whole of humanity and the impossibility of human compassion: "Poor, dear child, child of this world of delusion, of guilt, suffering, and of death; this world of eternal change, of disappointment, and of pain! May the Lord of Heaven be merciful to you on your journey."

LAST THINGS LAST

Strindberg's life was one of the most tormented and conflicted of modern times, but out of the dark vision that obsessed him arose some of the most exciting theater in the history of world drama. He strove to strip away hypocrisy and plunge into the dark, deep recesses of the mind and soul where sanity has no place, only the unending nightmare of disappointment and dread. If Strindberg had not existed one would have to wonder where Pirandello, Toller, Kaiser, O'Neill, Pinter, Ionesco, and Beckett would have come from, for they are his direct descendants. In the history of Western theater and among tragic dramatists, Strindberg takes his place with Aeschylus, Sophocles, Euripides, Shakespeare, Ibsen, and Chekhov.

DRAMATIC MOMENTS

from the Major Plays

These short excerpts are from the playwright's major plays. They give a taste of the work of the playwright. Each has a short introduction in brackets that helps the reader understand the context of the excerpt. The excerpts, which are in chronological order, illustrate the main themes mentioned in the In an Hour essay.

from **Miss Julie** (1888)

[Jean has just finished telling Miss Julie of his infatuation as a young boy with her and his distress at never being able to hope to rise into her class. The midsummer's night flirtation is about to become more serious, and then complicated by arrival of other people. Miss Julie's seduction and tragedy is underway, driven by complex motives and events.]

CHARACTERS

Miss Julie
Jean
Chorus

MISS JULIE: You have a really charming way of telling a story. Have you ever gone to school?

JEAN: Some. But I've read lots of novels and seen a good many plays. I've also listened to the talk of cultured people. I've learned most from that.

MISS JULIE: And what about us? Do you stand around listening to our conversations?

JEAN: Of course! And quite an earful I've gathered, too. From up on the carriage box, rowing the boat — once I heard you and one of your girl friends —

MISS JULIE: Is that so? And what did you hear, exactly?

JEAN: Oh, well, I — I really don't think I should tell. One thing surprised me, though, was where you'd learned all those words. When you get right down to it, I guess maybe there's not really so much difference between people and — people, as we think.

MISS JULIE: Shame on you! My class doesn't behave like yours when we're engaged!

JEAN: (*Looking at her.*) Are you so certain! Come, now, Miss Julie, you needn't play the innocent with me —

MISS JULIE: The man I offered my love to was shit.

JEAN: That's what you all say — afterwards.

MISS JULIE: All?

JEAN: I'd say so. I seem to have heard it before on similar occasions.

MISS JULIE: What occasions?

JEAN: The one we just spoke of. The last time —

MISS JULIE: (*Getting up.*) Shh! I don't want to hear anymore of this!

JEAN: Neither did she. Isn't it strange. — Well — if you'll excuse me, I'll go to bed.

MISS JULIE: (*Softly.*) Bed? On Midsummer Eve?

JEAN: Yes. Dancing with that rabble out there really has no attraction for me.

MISS JULIE: Get the key to the boathouse and row me out onto the lake. I want to see the sunrise.

JEAN: Is that wise?

MISS JULIE: Worried, are you? About your reputation?

JEAN: Why not? Why risk being made a fool of, getting sacked without a reference, and just when I'm on my way up in the world? Besides, I have a certain obligation to Kristin.

MISS JULIE: Ah, so it's Kristin now —

JEAN: Yes, but you as well. Take my advice, go upstairs, go to bed.

MISS JULIE: And since when do I take orders from you?

JEAN: This once. For your sake. It's late. Lack of sleep makes one drunk and the head dizzy. Go to bed. Besides — unless I'm mistaken — I hear the others coming to look for me. And if we're found here together, you're lost!

CHORUS: (*Heard approaching from the distance; under the following dialogue.*)

A lad and a lassie met in a wood
Tri-di-ri-di ral-la tri-di-ri-di-ra!
Come said the lassie let's do us what's good!
Tri-di-ri-di ral la la!

The lass she lay down beside the laddié

Tri-di-ri-di ral-la tri-di-ri-di-ra!

And said let us never be sad said she!

Tri-di-ri-di ral la la!

Then up she rose and donned her clothes

Tri-di-ri-di ral-la tri-di-ri-di-ra!

And went off sayin' that's how it goes!

Tri-di-ri-di ral la la!

MISS JULIE: I know these people, and I love them just as they love me. Let them come — you'll see.

JEAN: Love you, Miss Julie? No, they don't love you. They take your food and spit at you the minute you've turned your back. Believe me. Listen to them. Listen to what they're singing. — No, on second thought, don't listen.

MISS JULIE: (*Listening.*) What are they singing?

JEAN: Some nasty song about you and me —

MISS JULIE: How disgusting of them! The cowards — !

JEAN: Mobs are always cowardly! And since you can't fight them, the only thing is to run.

MISS JULIE: Run? Where to? There's no way out! And we can't go into Kristin's room —

JEAN: All right, then, into my room. This is no time to bother about conventions. You can trust me. I'm a true, loyal, and respectful friend.

MISS JULIE: But what — what if they look for you in there!

JEAN: I'll bolt the door. And if they try to break it down, I'll shoot! — Come! (*On his knees.*) Come!

MISS JULIE: (*Significantly.*) Do you promise me that —

JEAN: I promise! (*JEAN hurries after MISS JULIE who runs out to the right.*)

****

from **Playing with Fire** (1892)

[Husband and wife begin the circles of jealousy and desire, but there is room for others to play even if they are offstage taking a walk. Add a little salt to the wounds about the bourgeoisie and the playgoer has Strindberg's usual, but in this case comic, attacks.]

CHARACTERS

Knut
Kerstin
Mother
Father
Adèle

(A glass-enclosed verandah made over into a living room. Doors lead into the garden as well as right and left. KNUT is seated, painting. KERSTIN enters dressed casually for morning.)

KNUT: Is he up yet?

KERSTIN: Axel? How should I know?

KNUT: I thought you'd gone to check.

KERSTIN: Shame on you! If I didn't know you incapable of jealousy, I'd begin to wonder.

KNUT: And if I didn't know you incapable of infidelity, I'd be getting a little antsy.

KERSTIN: Why just now?

KNUT: Don't you listen? I said *if.* I value no one's company more than our friend Axel's. And since you share my feeling for the poor tormented soul, everything's fine.

KERSTIN: Yes, what a sad creature. Not to mention rather a bit odd from time to time. I mean, why did he take off so suddenly last summer, not a good-bye to be heard and left all his things?

KNUT: I admit, that was odd. I had the feeling he'd fallen in love with cousin Adèle.

KERSTIN: Did you?

KNUT: Yes. But I don't think so now. Mother thought he'd gone back to his wife and child.

KERSTIN: But why would he do such a thing? They're divorced.

KNUT: Not quite. He expects it to come through any day.

KERSTIN: I see. So you thought he was in love with Adèle? You should have told me. Actually I can see them getting along rather well together.

KNUT: Nonsense. Adèle's cold as a fish.

KERSTIN: Adèle? How would you know?

KNUT: She may have a lovely figure, but there's not an ounce of passion stirring in that body.

KERSTIN: Passion?

KNUT: Well, is there?

KERSTIN: Give her time. One day she'll break from that shell and —

KNUT: Do you think so?

KERSTIN: You sound interested.

KNUT: Well, maybe just a bit.

KERSTIN: Which bit?

KNUT: Don't forget, she modeled for me once, as The Swimmer —

KERSTIN: Yes, well, who hasn't? I just wish you wouldn't show your sketches to every passer-by. And here comes your mother.

(The MOTHER enters, dressed badly with a large Japanese hat and carrying a food basket.)

KNUT: Mother! You look an absolute fright today!

MOTHER: Oh, thank you very much!

KERSTIN: Knut will never learn manners. And what have you brought us for lunch?

MOTHER: Oh, I've found some lovely dabs.

KNUT: Oh, God, not dabs! *(Digging around in the basket.)* Bloody hell! What's this? Ducklings?

KERSTIN: They could have been a bit more plump. Feel the breasts.

KNUT: I think all breasts are lovely.

KERSTIN: Shame on you!

MOTHER: So, I see your friend turned up last night again.

KNUT: Kerstin's friend, not mine. She's the one who's crazy about him. When he arrived last night, I expected them to fall into each other's arms and kiss.

MOTHER: Don't joke like that, Knut. You know what they say about playing with fire.

KNUT: I know, I know, but I'm too old to start learning. Besides, look at me! Do I look like I need to worry?

MOTHER: It isn't a man's looks that count, is it, Kerstin?

KERSTIN: I don't know what on earth you're talking about.

MOTHER: *(Striking her lightly on the cheek.)* You just be careful, my dear!

KNUT: Kerstin hasn't an evil thought in her head. And you, you old bat, had better not start corrupting her.

MOTHER: You two and your nasty jokes! I never know when you're serious or not

KNUT: I'm always serious.

KERSTIN: I believe it. You don't laugh when you say these dreadful things.

MOTHER: You're certainly quarrelsome this morning. Didn't you two sleep well last night?

KNUT: Suppose we didn't sleep at all?

MOTHER: Oh, you wicked boy! Well, I guess I'd better be off, or your father'll start laying into me.

KNUT: Father, yes! Where is he?

MOTHER: On his morning walk with Adèle I should imagine.

KNUT: Aren't you jealous?

MOTHER: Oh, don't be silly!

KNUT: Well, I am.

MOTHER: Of what?

KNUT: The old man, who else?

MOTHER: Oh, Kerstin, Kerstin, what a family you've got yourself into!

KERSTIN: Well, I knew two things before I married him. First, I knew my Knut, and second, I knew artists are a crazy breed. Otherwise I wouldn't know heads from tails around here.

KNUT: At least I'm an artist. Father and mother are the lowest bourgeois parasites.

MOTHER: *(Without anger.)* No, my dear, it's you who are the parasite. You've never earned the cost of a crust of bread, and at your age! And your father was no bourgeois parasite when he built you this house. You're a lazy good-for-nothing!

KNUT: Oh, God, the life of an only son! Go, now, mother, go, before he comes and starts telling you off in here. It's not my favorite way of beginning the day. Hurry! Hurry up! He's coming!

MOTHER: I'll slip out this way then. *(She leaves.)*

KNUT: There's a bloody draft in this house that cuts right through you.

KERSTIN: Yes, and your parents might give us a bit more breathing space, a little peace now and then. We eat every meal with them, for God's sake.

KNUT: It's like feeding the sparrows on the sill. As long as you feed them, you like to see the little dears eat.

KERSTIN: *(Listens.)* Shh! Cheer the old man up. It might save us the morning row.

KNUT: Don't I wish! He's not always in the mood for my jokes.

(The FATHER enters dressed in a white waistcoat and black velvet jacket, a rose in his buttonhole. ADÈLE enters and after walking about for awhile begins dusting.)

****

from **A Dream Play** (1901)

[The lawyer and Indra's Daughter, who is exploring human misery, begin with hope. Time and space change in dreamlike sequences, and what began in hope becomes an exploration of entrapment and hate.]

CHARACTERS

> Lawyer
> Daughter
> Kristin
> Officer

(The stage grows dark. The DAUGHTER rises and goes to the LAWYER. A change in lighting transforms the organ into Fingal's Cave. The sea surges in under the basalt columns. The wind and the waves combine in a great harmonious sound.)

LAWYER: Where are we, sister?

DAUGHTER: What do you hear?

LAWYER: Drops falling —

DAUGHTER: The tears of mankind weeping. What else do you hear?

LAWYER: Sighing — moaning — wailing —

DAUGHTER: Man's cries reach this far, no farther. But why this eternal lament? Is there no joy in life?

LAWYER: Yes — the sweetest that is also the bitterest. Love! Marriage and a home! The highest and the lowest!

DAUGHTER: I have to try!

LAWYER: With me?

DAUGHTER: With you! You know the rocks and dangerous places. We'll avoid them.

LAWYER: But I'm poor.

DAUGHTER: Does that matter, as long as we love each other? A little beauty costs nothing.

42

LAWYER: I hate things that you might love.

DAUGHTER: Then we'll compromise.

LAWYER: And when we grow tired of each other?

DAUGHTER: We'll have a child who will bring us happiness that will never grow old.

LAWYER: You'll take me as I am? Poor, ugly, despised, rejected?

DAUGHTER: Yes! We'll join our destinies!

LAWYER: So be it!

(A very simple room beside the LAWYER's office. At the right is a large bed with a canopy; beside it a window. To the left is an iron stove with cooking utensils. KRISTIN is busy applying strips of paper along the joints of the inner window. A glass door in the background leads into the office; behind it we see a number of poorly dressed PEOPLE waiting to be admitted.)

KRISTIN: I'm pasting, I'm pasting!

DAUGHTER: (*Pale and worn, sitting at the stove.*) You're shutting out the air! I'm suffocating —

KRISTIN: There's only a small crack left.

DAUGHTER: Air, air! I can't breathe!

KRISTIN: I'm pasting, I'm pasting!

LAWYER: That's right, Kristin! Heat is costly!

DAUGHTER: It's as if you were pasting my mouth shut!

LAWYER: (*In the doorway, a document in his hand.*) Is the baby sleeping?

DAUGHTER: Yes, finally!

LAWYER: (*Softly.*) His screaming drives my clients away.

DAUGHTER: (*Gently.*) What can we do about it?

LAWYER: Nothing.

DAUGHTER: We'll have to find a larger apartment.

LAWYER: We haven't any money.

DAUGHTER: May I open the window? The air in here is making me choke.

LAWYER: The heat will escape and we'll freeze.

DAUGHTER: It's horrible! Can't we at least scrub the floor out there?

LAWYER: You aren't strong enough, and neither am I. And Kristin has to go on pasting. She has to paste the whole house shut. Every crack in the floor, the walls, the ceiling.

DAUGHTER: I was prepared for poverty, not for dirt.

LAWYER: Poverty is always relatively dirty.

DAUGHTER: It's worse than I ever dreamed.

LAWYER: It could be worse. There's still food in the pot.

DAUGHTER: You call that food?

LAWYER: Cabbage is cheap, nourishing, and good.

DAUGHTER: If you like cabbage. I can't stand it.

LAWYER: Why didn't you say so?

DAUGHTER: Because I loved you. I wanted to sacrifice for you.

LAWYER: Then I'll have to sacrifice my love for cabbage. Sacrifices must be mutual.

DAUGHTER: Then what will we eat? Fish? You hate fish.

LAWYER: It's also expensive.

DAUGHTER: Life is harder than I ever dreamed.

LAWYER: (*Gently.*) Yes, now you see how hard it is. And the child who was to have been our bond and blessing has become our ruin.

DAUGHTER: Oh, my dear! I'm dying in this air, in this room with its view of the yard, and the child's endless screaming, keeping me awake, and those people out there with their wailing and quarreling and accusations! I'll die in this room!

LAWYER: Poor little flower! Without light, without air —

DAUGHTER: And you say there are those who are worse off —

LAWYER: I'm one of the most envied men in the neighborhood.

DAUGHTER: I could bear it if only I had some beauty in here.

LAWYER: I know — I know what you mean — a flower — a heliotrope especially. But that costs one and a half — that's six bottles of milk or half a bushel of potatoes.

DAUGHTER: I'd gladly do without food if only I had my flower.

LAWYER: There's a kind of beauty that costs nothing. Not to have it is the worst torture for a man with any sense of beauty.

DAUGHTER: And what's that?

LAWYER: No, you'll get angry.

DAUGHTER: We agreed never to be angry.

LAWYER: We agreed — yes — I know. Everything will be all right, Agnes, if only there are no hard words. Do you know what I mean? No, not yet!

DAUGHTER: And there never will be.

LAWYER: Never, as long as it depends on me.

DAUGHTER: Go on.

LAWYER: Well — whenever I go into a house the first thing I notice is how the curtains are hanging. (*He goes to the curtains at the window and puts them in order.*) And if they're hanging crooked and look like rags — I leave. And then I look at the chairs. If they're in their proper places, I stay. (*He pushes a chair to the wall.*) Then I look at the candles in their holders. If they're crooked, the whole house is a mess. (*He straightens the candles on the sideboard.*) And so you see, my dear, there's the beauty that costs nothing.

DAUGHTER: (*Drops her head.*) Those are hard words, Axel!

LAWYER: They're not!

DAUGHTER: They *are!*

LAWYER: The hell with it!

DAUGHTER: What kind of language is that?

LAWYER: I'm sorry, Agnes. But I've suffered as much from your slovenliness as you have from the dirt. And I didn't dare put things straight for fear you'd get mad and think I was scolding you. Ugh! Shall we stop this now?

DAUGHTER: Why is marriage so hard? Can there be anything harder? One has to be an angel to survive.

LAWYER: I know.

DAUGHTER: I think I'm beginning to hate you!

LAWYER: Then I pity us. But let's keep hatred out of it. I promise you,

Agnes, I'll never complain of your housekeeping again, no matter if it tortures me.

DAUGHTER: And I'll eat cabbage, no matter if it tortures me.

LAWYER: A life together in agony, then. One's pleasure, the other's pain!

DAUGHTER: Alas for mankind!

LAWYER: You understand that now?

DAUGHTER: Yes. But in God's name let's avoid the rocks. We know them so well by now.

LAWYER: Yes. All right. We'll do that. After all, we're humane, enlightened people. We can forgive and forget.

DAUGHTER: We can even smile at trifles.

LAWYER: We can. Yes, we can. — You know, I read in the paper this morning — by the way, where is the paper?

DAUGHTER: (*Embarrassed.*) Which paper?

LAWYER: (*Harshly.*) Do I take more than one paper?

DAUGHTER: Smile — don't be so hard. — I used it to light the fire this morning.

LAWYER: (*Violently.*) The hell you did!

DAUGHTER: Smile! — I burned it because it ridiculed what is sacred to me.

LAWYER: And what is *not* sacred to *me!* Hm! (*Slams his fist into his other hand furiously.*) I'll smile! I'll smile till my molars show! I'll be considerate, I'll hide my thoughts, I'll say yes to everything, I'll evade it all and play the hypocrite! All right, so you've burned the paper. Well, well — (*Straightens the curtains at the bed.*) There, I'm straightening up again, and you'll lose your temper. — Oh, Agnes, this is impossible!

DAUGHTER: I know, I know —

LAWYER: But we'll go on, not because of our vows, but for the child.

DAUGHTER: Yes. For the child. — We *must* go on, we *must* —

LAWYER: I have to get back to my clients. Listen to them. Mumbling with impatience. Can't wait to tear one another to pieces, get each other fined and thrown into prison — lost souls —

DAUGHTER: Poor unhappy people. And this pasting! (*Lowers her head in silent despair.*)

KRISTIN: I'm pasting, I'm pasting!

(*The LAWYER stands at the door, nervously fingering the handle.*)

DAUGHTER: Oh, the squeal of that doorknob! It's like you were twisting my heart in your fist —

LAWYER: I'm twisting, I'm twisting —

DAUGHTER: Don't!

LAWYER: I'm twisting —

DAUGHTER: No!

LAWYER: I —

OFFICER: (*Enters from the office, taking hold of the door handle.*) May I intrude?

LAWYER: (*Lets loose of the handle.*) Of course! Since you have your degree now!

OFFICER: And all the world is mine! All paths open to me! Parnassus scaled, laurels won, immortality and fame! Everything, mine!

LAWYER: How will you live?

OFFICER: Live?

LAWYER: You'll need a roof over your head, clothes, food?

OFFICER: No problem when there's someone who loves you.

LAWYER: Imagine that! Imagine! — Paste, Kristin, paste! Till they can't breathe. (*Goes out backwards, nodding.*)

KRISTIN: I'm pasting, I'm pasting! Till they can't breathe!

OFFICER: Will you come with me now?

DAUGHTER: Yes! Now! But where?

OFFICER: To Fairhaven. It's summer there, the sun's shining, youth and children and flowers! Singing, dancing, feasting, rejoicing!

DAUGHTER: I want to go there!

OFFICER: Come!

LAWYER: (*Reenters.*) I'll go back to my first hell. This was the second, and the greatest. The most beautiful hell is always the greatest. — Look at this, she's left hairpins lying on the floor again. (*Picks one up.*)

OFFICER: Good Lord, he's found the hairpins, too.

LAWYER: Too? Look at this one. Two prongs, but one pin. Two and yet one. Straighten it and it becomes one. Bend it again and it's two, without ever ceasing to be one. That is to say, two are one! And yet if I break it — like this — then the two are two. (*Breaks the hairpin and throws the pieces away.*)

OFFICER: So he understands it all! — But before you can break it, the two prongs must diverge. If they converge, then it holds.

LAWYER: And if they're parallel — they'll never meet. It neither holds nor breaks.

OFFICER: The hairpin! The most perfect of created objects! A straight line which at the same time is two parallels!

LAWYER: A lock that closes when it's open!

OFFICER: Like this door. In closing it I open the way for you, Agnes. (*Goes out and closes the door.*)

DAUGHTER: And now?

****

from **The Dance of Death Part I** (1901)
from Act One

[The conversation between the Captain and his wife begins benignly enough, but the descent into the hellishness of their marriage is swift and relentless, always down and always worse.]

CHARACTERS

> Captain
>
> Alice
>
> Jenny

CAPTAIN: Won't you play something for me?

ALICE: *(Indifferent, but not snappish.)* What shall I play?

CAPTAIN: Whatever you like.

ALICE: You don't like my repertoire.

CAPTAIN: Nor you mine.

ALICE: *(Changing the subject.)* Do you want the doors left open?

CAPTAIN: Suit yourself.

ALICE: Let them be, then. *(Pause.)* You're not smoking?

CAPTAIN: Strong tobacco is giving me problems.

ALICE: *(Almost friendly.)* Then smoke something milder. As you say, it's your only pleasure.

CAPTAIN: Pleasure? I don't understand.

ALICE: Why ask me? I know as little as you. Aren't you having your whiskey?

CAPTAIN: I'll wait a bit. What's for dinner?

ALICE: How should I know? Ask Kristin.

CAPTAIN: Shouldn't mackerel be in season soon. It *is* autumn.

ALICE: Yes, it's autumn.

CAPTAIN: Outside *and* in. But leaving aside the cold that comes with autumn, both outside and in, a nice piece of grilled mackerel with a slice of lemon and a glass of white burgundy is not wholly to be despised.

ALICE: Mercy! Such eloquence!

CAPTAIN: Is there any burgundy left in the wine-cellar?

ALICE: It's news to me we've *had* a wine-cellar these past five years.

CAPTAIN: You've never kept stock of things. In any case, we'll need to put some up for our silver wedding —

ALICE: Are you really going to celebrate that?

CAPTAIN: Naturally.

ALICE: It might be more natural to keep our misery to ourselves. Our twenty-five years of misery —

CAPTAIN: Dear Alice. Misery we most assuredly have had, but there's also been fun now and again. It's better to use the little time we have left, for once it's over, it's over.

ALICE: Over. If only it were.

CAPTAIN: You can count on it. Scarcely enough left to cart out in a wheelbarrow and spread across the garden.

ALICE: All this trouble for a garden.

CAPTAIN: That's life. Don't blame me.

ALICE: All this trouble. *(Pause.)* Has the mail come?

CAPTAIN: Yes.

ALICE: The butcher's bill?

CAPTAIN: Yes.

ALICE: What was it?

CAPTAIN: *(Takes a paper from his pocket and puts on his glasses, then immediately takes them off.)* Look for yourself. I can't see any more —

ALICE: What's wrong with your eyes?

CAPTAIN: Don't know.

ALICE: Age.

CAPTAIN: Nonsense! Me?

ALICE: Well, not me.

CAPTAIN: Hm!

ALICE: *(Looking at the bill.)* Can you pay it?

CAPTAIN: Yes. Just not now.

ALICE: Ah, well, later, then. In a year, perhaps, when you're retired on a small pension, and it's too late. When your illness returns —

CAPTAIN: Illness? I've never been ill. Except that once, and that was only a slight indisposition. I'll live another twenty years.

ALICE: Not according to the doctor.

CAPTAIN: Doctor!

ALICE: Who would know better? Hm?

CAPTAIN: Nothing wrong with me. Never has been, and never will be. I'll die the death of an old soldier. Suddenly.

ALICE: Speaking of the doctor — he's giving a party this evening, you know.

CAPTAIN: (*Agitated.*) So? We're not invited because we don't associate with them, and we don't associate with them because we don't want to, and we don't want to because I despise their guts. Both of them. They're scum.

ALICE: You say that about everyone.

CAPTAIN: Because everyone's scum.

ALICE: Except you.

CAPTAIN: Yes. I have behaved decently, no matter what. *That's* why I'm not scum.

(*Pause.*)

ALICE: Do you want to play cards?

CAPTAIN: Why not.

(*ALICE takes a pack of cards from the drawer of the sewing table and starts to shuffle them.*)

ALICE: Just think of it. The doctor's having the military band. For a private party.

CAPTAIN: (*Angry.*) That's because he sucks up to the Colonel in town! Sucks up, you hear? If only *I'd* been able —

ALICE: *(Dealing.)* I was friends once with Gerda, but she let me down —

CAPTAIN: They're all cheats, every one of them! What's trumps?

ALICE: Put on your glasses.

CAPTAIN: They don't help. *(Sighs.)* Well? Well?

ALICE: Spades are trumps.

CAPTAIN: *(Annoyed.)* Spades?

ALICE: *(Playing.)* Yes, you may be right. They've written us off in any case — the new officers' wives.

CAPTAIN: *(Playing and taking the trick.)* So what? We don't give parties, so we won't notice. I can be alone. Always have been.

ALICE: So have I. But the children. The children are growing up knowing no one.

CAPTAIN: They can find their own friends in town. My trick! Any trumps left?

ALICE: One. That was mine!

CAPTAIN: Six and eight makes fifteen —

ALICE: Fourteen! Fourteen!

CAPTAIN: Six and eight makes fourteen. I appear to have forgotten how to count, as well. And two makes sixteen. *(Yawns.)* Your deal.

ALICE: Tired?

CAPTAIN: *(Dealing.)* Not in the least.

ALICE: *(Listening.)* You can hear the music all this way. *(Pause.)* Do you think Kurt's been invited?

CAPTAIN: He got in this morning, so he's had time to unpack his dress suit, but no time to drop in on us —

ALICE: Quarantine Officer? Will there be a Quarantine Station here?

CAPTAIN: Yes.

ALICE: After all, he *is* my cousin — we once even shared the same name —

CAPTAIN: Nothing to be proud of there —

ALICE: Now you listen. *(Sharply.)* Just you leave my family alone, and I'll leave yours!

CAPTAIN: All right, all right! Let's not start that again!

ALICE: Is the Quarantine Officer a doctor?

CAPTAIN: No. He's a sort of civil servant in the administration, a book-keeper. Kurt never made anything of himself.

ALICE: Life hasn't been easy for him —

CAPTAIN: And he's cost us a pretty penny. And to desert his wife and children as he did was an unheard of scandal.

ALICE: No need to be so harsh, Edgar.

CAPTAIN: It's true. And what's he been up to since — in America, eh? Can't exactly say I miss him. He was a nice enough boy, though, I liked arguing with him.

ALICE: Because he always gave in.

CAPTAIN: (Haughtily.) Gave in or not, he at least was a person I could talk to. There's not a person on this island who understands a word I say. It's a community of idiots!

ALICE: How odd Kurt should turn up just now, for our silver wedding — whether we celebrate it or not.

CAPTAIN: Odd? Why? Ah, yes, of course. It was he who brought us together — married you off, as they say.

ALICE: Well, didn't he?

CAPTAIN: Oh, no question. Got this idea in his head. I leave it for you to judge its merits.

ALICE: A foolish whim —

CAPTAIN: Which we've been paying for ever since. Not he.

ALICE: Yes. Just imagine if I'd stayed on at the theater. My friends are all stars now.

CAPTAIN: (Rising.) Ah, yes. I think I'll have my whiskey. (He goes to the cupboard and mixes a drink, which he takes standing.) There ought to be a rail here to rest one's foot on. I could imagine I was in Copenhagen at the American Bar.

ALICE: Ah, yes, a rail, to remind us of Copenhagen. After all, we did spend our best moments there.

CAPTAIN: *(Taking a long drink.)* Yes. Do you recall that *navarin aux pommes* at Nim's Restaurant? *(He smacks his lips.)*

ALICE: No. But I remember the concerts at Tivoli.

CAPTAIN: Such cultivated tastes you have.

ALICE: You should be glad having a wife with good taste.

CAPTAIN: Oh, I am.

ALICE: For those times when you need to brag about her.

CAPTAIN: *(Drinking.)* They must be dancing at the doctor's. I can hear the three-quarter time of the tuba's. *Boom*-boom-boom.

ALICE: I hear the Alcazar Waltz. It wasn't yesterday I last danced a waltz —

CAPTAIN: Can you still?

ALICE: Still?

CAPTAIN: Yes — well, I mean, you're a bit past your dancing days. Same as me, I'd say.

ALICE: But I'm ten years younger than you.

CAPTAIN: In which case, we're the same age, since the wife is always ten years younger.

ALICE: Shame on you. You're an old goat, and I'm in my prime.

CAPTAIN: Oh, yes, certainly — you can still be charming — to others, when you put your mind to it.

ALICE: May we light the lamp now?

CAPTAIN: Be my guest.

ALICE: You'll ring?

(The CAPTAIN walks slowly to the desk and rings. JENNY enters from the right.)

CAPTAIN: Would you kindly light the lamp, please, Jenny?

ALICE: *(Sharply.)* Light the hanging lamp.

JENNY: Yes, ma'am. *(She lights the hanging lamp while the CAPTAIN watches.)*

ALICE: *(Curtly.)* Have you wiped the chimney properly?

JENNY: As much as it needs.

ALICE: What kind of answer is that?

CAPTAIN: Now — now —

ALICE: *(To JENNY.)* Get out! I'll light it myself.

JENNY: Yes, I think so, too. *(Going to the door.)*

ALICE: *(Rising.)* Go!

JENNY: *(Stops.)* And what would you do if I did, I wonder?

(ALICE is silent. JENNY goes out. The CAPTAIN lights the lamp.)

ALICE: *(Uneasy.)* Do you think she'll leave?

CAPTAIN: Wouldn't surprise me in the least. What a pickle we'd be in then.

ALICE: It's your fault. You spoil them.

CAPTAIN: I do no such thing. They're always polite to me.

ALICE: Because you're their toady. You toady to everyone who's your inferior. Like every despot, at heart you're a slave.

CAPTAIN: Now — now —

ALICE: You toady to *them*, yes, to your men, to the noncommissioned officers. But when it comes to your equals and superiors, you simply can't get along with them.

CAPTAIN: Ugh!

ALICE: Like all tyrants. Do you think she'll leave?

CAPTAIN: Yes, if you don't go and say something nice to her.

ALICE: Me?

CAPTAIN: If I did it you'd say I was flirting with the maids.

ALICE: Just imagine if she goes. I'd have to do the housework myself, like the last time, and my hands would be ruined.

CAPTAIN: That's not the worst of it. If Jenny goes, so will Kristin, and we'll never get another servant to the island. The steamer pilot scares off anyone who comes looking for a position, and if *he* misses his chance, my gunners will do it.

ALICE: Your gunners, yes, that I have to feed in my kitchen because you haven't the guts to show them the door.

CAPTAIN: And if I did, they'd leave when their term was up and I'd have to close down the gunshop.

ALICE: That would ruin us!

CAPTAIN: Which is why the officers are petitioning the government for supplementary pay —

ALICE: Who for?

CAPTAIN: For the gunners.

ALICE: *(Laughing.)* You're out of your mind.

CAPTAIN: Laugh a little for me while you're at it. I could use it.

ALICE: Soon I'll have forgotten how to laugh —

CAPTAIN: *(Lighting a cigar.)* That's something never to forget. It's tedious enough as it is.

ALICE: Well, it's certainly not amusing. Shall we go on playing?

CAPTAIN: No, it's tiring.

(Pause.)

ALICE: Still, it does annoy me, you know, that my cousin, our new Quarantine Officer, calls on our enemies before visiting us.

CAPTAIN: Oh, why bother yourself over it.

ALICE: Did you see in the newspaper that he was described as a man of independent means? He must have come into some money.

CAPTAIN: Independent means! My-my! A rich relation. That's a first for this family.

ALICE: Your family, yes, mine has had many who were wealthy.

CAPTAIN: If he's come into money, he's bound to be on his high horse. But I'll keep him in check. He won't be getting a look at *my* cards.

(The telegraph apparatus begins clicking out a message. The CAPTAIN rises.)

ALICE: Who could that be?

CAPTAIN: *(Stands still.)* Quiet a moment, please!

ALICE: Go over and see.

CAPTAIN: I hear. I hear what they're saying. It's the children. *(He goes to the apparatus and taps out a response. The apparatus responds. The CAPTAIN responds.)*

ALICE: Well?

CAPTAIN: No, wait! *(He gives a final tap.)* It was the children. They're at the guardhouse in town. Judith's not feeling well again and staying away from school.

ALICE: Again? And?

CAPTAIN: Money, what else.

ALICE: Why is Judith in such a hurry? If she takes her exams next year, that's time enough.

CAPTAIN: Tell her. See what good it does.

ALICE: You should tell her.

CAPTAIN: How many times *haven't* I told her? Children do as they please, as you very well know.

ALICE: At least they do in *this* house. *(The CAPTAIN yawns.)* Is it necessary to yawn in your wife's presence?

CAPTAIN: What would you suggest? Doesn't it occur to you that day in, day out we say the same things to each other? Just now when you sprang that well-worn phrase of yours: "At least they do in *this* house," my cue was to dredge up my standard response: "It's not only *my* house." But since I have used that response five hundred times already, I yawned instead. My yawn could be taken to mean that I am too lazy to respond, or: "You're right, my angel," or: "Can't we just stop this nonsense!"

ALICE: Your charm is especially acute this evening.

CAPTAIN: Isn't it time for dinner soon?

ALICE: Did you know the doctor ordered dinner from the Grand Hotel in town?

CAPTAIN: No! Then they'll be having hazel hens. Ah, what birds! The best! But it's barbaric to fry them in pork grease.

ALICE: Must we talk about food?

CAPTAIN: Well, in that case, wine. I wonder what the barbarians are drinking with their hazel hen?

ALICE: Shall I play for you?

CAPTAIN: (*Seating himself at the desk.*) The last resort. Yes, if only you could steer clear of your funeral marches and lamentations. It sounds as if you're trying to teach a moral lesson with music. I'm quite capable of filling in for myself the obvious message lurking beneath: "Hear what misery is mine! Meow, meow! Here what a dreadful husband I have! Brum, brum, brum! Oh, if only he were dead!" Fanfares! The joyous roll of drums! And end with the Alcazar Waltz! The Champagne Galop! Speaking of champagne, I'm certain there are two bottles left. Why not bring them up and pretend we have company?

ALICE: We certainly will not; they're mine. I got them as gifts.

CAPTAIN: What a sense of economy!

ALICE: As economical as you are stingy — at least toward your wife.

CAPTAIN: Then I'm afraid I'm out of ideas. Shall I dance for you?

ALICE: Thank you, no. *Your* dancing days are done.

CAPTAIN: What you need is a female companion to live with you.

ALICE: Thanks! And what you need is a male companion to live with you.

CAPTAIN: Thanks. We tried that. To our mutual dissatisfaction. But it was interesting, all the same. As soon as there was an outsider in the house we were happy — at least for a time.

ALICE: But afterward!

CAPTAIN: Oh, let's not talk about it.

****

from **The Ghost Sonata** (1907)

[The setup for vengeance is complete. The Old Man and the Colonel are face-to-face, but events do not unfold as expected. The mummy appears and complicates everything. Time, life, and death are suspended and resumed in this dream sequence. Meantime the playgoers are confronted with the dangers to life, exuberant and enjoyable, that lie in us all.]

CHARACTERS

> Milkmaid
>
> Colonel
>
> Mummy
>
> Bengtsson
>
> Johansson
>
> Daughter
>
> Student

(All sit silently in a circle.)

COLONEL: Shall we have some tea?

OLD MAN: Tea? Why? No one likes tea, so why pretend! (*Pause.*)

COLONEL: Then shall we talk?

OLD MAN: (*Slowly and with pauses.*) About what? The weather? But we know that. Ask how we're all doing? We know that, too. I prefer silence. In silence we see thoughts. In silence we see the past. Silence conceals nothing. Words conceal. I read recently that language differences arose among primitive savage tribes — they needed to keep tribal secrets private and unknown to rival tribes. Languages, therefore, are codes, and whoever finds the key will understand all the world's languages. Not that secrets can't be discovered without a key. Particularly in cases where proof of paternity is at issue. Legal proof, of course, is another matter. Two false witnesses testifying in court are sufficient, as long as their testimonies agree. But in such cases as I have in mind no witnesses are possible. Nature herself has endowed man with a sense of shame which attempts to hide what ought to be hidden. At times, of course, without willing it, we slip into situations, in which, at times, by chance, the most secret of secrets must be revealed, where the mask is torn from the impostor, and where the villain is exposed. (*Pause. They all look at one another in silence.*) How quiet it has become. (*Long silence.*) Here, for example, in this respectable house, in this elegant home, where wealth and culture and beauty are united. (*Long silence.*) All of us sitting here know who we are. Do we not? No need for me to tell you. And each of you knows me, although you pretend not to. And sitting in that room is my daughter — *my* daughter, yes — as you also know. She's lost her desire to live and doesn't know why. She's withered away in this air polluted with crime and deception and lies of every kind. That's why I've searched to find her a friend, a friend in whose presence she may once again experience the light and the warmth that emanate from a noble deed. (*Long silence.*) That was my aim in this house. To pull up weeds, to unmask crimes, to settle accounts, so that these young people can make a new beginning, a new life in this home, which is my gift to them. (*Long silence.*) Each of you will now depart in peace and safe conduct, and whoever stays behind will be arrested. (*Long silence.*) Listen to the ticking, ticking of the clock. Like the ticking of the deathwatch beetle in the wall. Do you hear what it says? "Time-is-up! Time-is-up!" When it strikes — in another moment — your time will be up. Then you may go — not before. But before it strikes, it threatens you. Listen! It's warning! "The clock-can-strike!" And I can strike, too! (*He strikes the table with one of his crutches.*) Do you hear? (*Silence.*)

MUMMY: (*Goes to the clock and stops it; then speaks clearly and seriously.*) But I can stop time in its course. I can undo the past, make what is done undone. But not with threats and bribes — but through suffering and repentance. (*She goes to the OLD MAN.*) We are weak and miserable creatures; we know that. We have erred, we have sinned, the same as all the others. We are not what we seem, for at bottom we are better than what we believe, because we despise and condemn our sins. But when you, Jacob Hummel, with your false name, set yourself up to judge us, you prove you are worse and more contemptible than we who are miserable! You are not who you seem to be! You are a thief of the souls of men! You once stole me with false promises, just as you murdered the consul here we buried today, strangled him with his debts; and you stole that student's soul by binding him to you with an imaginary debt of his father's, who never owed you a cent. (*The OLD MAN has attempted to rise and speak; but he crumples back into his chair and shrinks smaller and smaller as she continues.*) But there is a dark spot in your life that I don't know the full truth of, though I have my suspicions. But I suspect Bengtsson knows. (*She rings the bell on the table.*)

OLD MAN: No! Not Bengtsson! Not him!

MUMMY: Then he *does* know! (*She rings again. The MILKMAID appears in the door to the hallway. She is visible to no one but the OLD MAN who is struck with horror. At BENGTSSON's entrance, the MILKMAID disappears.*) Bengtsson, do you know this person?

BENGTSSON: Yes, and he knows me. Life has its ups and downs, as you must know. I was in his service once and he in mine. For two whole years he sponged food from my kitchen — he was the cook's boy friend. Since he had to leave at three, dinner had to be ready at two, so for the sake of this ox we had to be satisfied with his warmed leftovers. But he drank the soup stock, too; what was left had to be eked out with water. He sat outside like a vampire sucking the marrow from the house so that we became skeletons. And he very nearly had us thrown in jail, because we accused the cook of being a thief.—I met this man later in Hamburg. He had another name. He'd become a loan shark, a bloodsucker. It was there he was accused of having lured a young girl out onto the ice to drown her— she'd witnessed a crime he was afraid would come to light.

MUMMY: (*Passes her hand over the face of the OLD MAN.*) This is who you are! Now give me the promissory notes and your will! (*JOHANSSON appears in the door to the hallway and watches the proceedings with great interest, with the knowledge that he is about to be freed from slavery. The OLD MAN extracts the packet of papers from his pocket and throws it on the table. The MUMMY strokes the OLD MAN's back.*) Polly! — Is that you, Jacob?

OLD MAN: (*Like a parrot.*) Jacob is here! Pretty-pretty Polly!

MUMMY: Can the clock strike?

OLD MAN: The clock can strike! (*Imitating a cuckoo clock.*) Cuckoo! Cuckoo! Cuckoo!

MUMMY: (*Opening the door to the closet.*) Now the clock has struck! Get up! Go into the closet where I have sat for twenty years mourning our sin! In there you will find a rope hanging. Let it represent the rope you used to strangle the consul up there, and with which you intended to strangle your benefactor. Go! (*The OLD MAN enters the closet. The MUMMY closes the door.*) Bengtsson! Set up the screen! The death screen!

(*BENGTSSON sets up the death screen in front of the door.*)

ALL: Amen!

(*Long silence.—In the Hyacinth Room the DAUGHTER sits at a harp and, after a prelude, accompanies the STUDENT's recitation of a song.*)

STUDENT: I saw the sun, and so it seemed
    That I beheld the Hidden One
    Whose works must give us joy.
    Blessèd the man who works for good!
    Never seek to right with evil
    Deeds that you have done in anger.
    Comfort whom you have afflicted,
    Through kindness will the grievance heal.
    Innocence is free of fear.
    The innocent is blest.

****

Strindberg

THE READING ROOM

YOUNG ACTORS AND THEIR TEACHERS

Anderson, Ingvar. *A History of Sweden*. London: Weidenfels and Nicolson, 1956.

Campbell, G. A. *Strindberg*. New York: Macmillan, 1933.

Lamm, Martin. *Modern Drama*. Oxford: Blackwell, 1952.

_____. *August Strindberg*. New York: Blom, 1971.

Meyer, Michael. *File on Strindberg*. London and New York: Methuen, 1986.

Mortensen, Brita, and Brian Downs. *Strindberg: An Introduction to His Life and Work*. Cambridge: Cambridge University Press, 1949.

Valency, Maurice. *The Flower and the Castle: An Introduction to Modern Drama*. New York and London: Macmillan, 1963.

SCHOLARS, STUDENTS, PROFESSORS

Anderson, Hans. *Strindberg's Master Olof and Shakespeare*. Uppsala. Sweden: Almqvist & Wiksell, 1952.

Antoine, André. *Memories of the Théâtre Libre*. Coral Gables, Fla.: University of Miami Press, 1964.

Bentley, Eric. *In Search of Theater*. New York: Vintage, 1954.

_____. *The Playwright as Thinker*. New York: Meridian, 1960.

Borland, Harold. *Nietzsche's Influence on Swedish Literature with Special Reference to Strindberg, Ola Hansson, Heidenstam and Fröding*. Göteborg, Sweden: Wettergren & Kerber, 1956.

Brandell, Gunnar. *Strindberg in Inferno*. Cambridge: Harvard University Press, Mass. 1974.

Carlson, Harry G. *Strindberg and the Poetry of Myth*. Berkeley and Los Angeles: University of California Press, 1982.

This extensive bibliography lists books about the playwright according to whom the books might be of interest. If you would like to research further something that interests you in the text, lists of references, sources cited, and editions used in this book are found in this section.

Carter, Lawson A. *Zola and the Theatre.* New Haven, Conn.: Yale University Press, 1963.

Dahlström, Carl E. W. L. *Strindberg's Dramatic Expressionism.* 2nd ed. New York: Blom, 1965.

Elovson, Harald, "August Strindberg and Emigration to America Until ca. 1890." *Scandinavian-American Interrelations.* Oslo: Universitetsforlaget, 1971.

Englund, Claes, and Gunnel Bergström, eds. *Strindberg, O'Neill, and the Modern Theatre: Addresses and Discussions at a Nobel Symposium at the Royal Dramatic Theatre, Stockholm.* Stockholm: Nobel Foundation and the Royal Dramatic Theatre, 1990.

McGill, V. J. *August Strindberg, the Bedeviled Viking.* New York: Russell and Russell, 1930.

Østerud, Erik. *Theatrical and Narrative Space: Studies in Ibsen, Strindberg and J. P. Jacobsen.* Aarhus, Denmark: Aarhus University Press, 1998.

Palmblad, Harry. *Strindberg's Conception of History.* New York: Columbia University Press, 1927.

Perridon, Harry, ed. *Strindberg, Ibsen, and Bergman: Essays on Scandinavian Film and Drama.* Maastricht, Netherlands: Shaker Press, 1998.

Reinert, Otto, ed. *Strindberg: Critical Essays.* Englewood Cliffs, N.J.: Prentice-Hall, 1971.

Robinson, Michael. *Strindberg and Photography: Writing and Living a Life.* Norwich, UK: Norvik Press, 1986.

―――――, ed. *Strindberg and Genre.* Norwich, UK: Norvik Press, 1991.

―――――. *Studies in Strindberg.* Norwich, UK: Norvik Press, 1998.

Rokem, Freddie. *Strindberg's Secret Codes.* Norwich, UK: Norvik Press, 2004.

Rossel, Hakon, and Michael Robinson, eds. *Expressionism and Modernism: New Approaches to August Strindberg.* Wien: Edition Praesens, 1999.

Steene, Birgitta. *The Greatest Fire: A Study of August Strindberg.* Carbondale: Southern Illinois University Press, 1973.

Stockenström, Göran, ed. *Strindberg's Dramaturgy.* Minneapolis: University of Minnesota Press, 1988.

Strindberg, August. *Letters of Strindberg to Harriet Bosse.* New York: Nelson, 1959.

―――――. *Open Letters to the Intimate Theater.* Seattle: University of Washington Press, 1959.

―――――. *From an Occult Diary.* New York: Hill and Wang, 1965.

Strindberg, Frida. *Marriage with Genius*. London: Cape, 1937.

Swerling, Anthony, ed. *In Quest of Strindberg*. Cambridge: Trinity Lane Press, 1971.

_____. *Strindberg's Impact on France, 1920–1960*. Cambridge: Trinity Lane Press, 1971.

Toksvig, Signe. *Emmanuel Swedenborg, Scientist and Mystic*. New Haven, Conn.: Yale University Press, 1949.

THEATER, PRODUCERS

Brustein, Robert. *The Theatre of Revolt*. Boston: Little Brown, 1964.

Esslin, Martin. *The Theatre of the Absurd*. Garden City, N.Y.: Doubleday, 1961.

Gassner, John. *Masters of the Drama*. New York: Dover, 1945.

Gunnar, Ollen. *August Strindberg*. New York: Unger, 1972.

Klaf, Franklin. *Strindberg, The Origin of Psychology in Modern Drama*. New York: Citadel Press, 1963.

Madsen, Børge G. *Strindberg's Naturalistic Theatre: Its Relationship to French Naturalism*. New York: Russell & Russell, 1973.

Marker, Lise-Lone. *The Scandinavian Theatre: A Short History*. Oxford: Blackwell, 1975.

Upvall, Axel Johan. *August Strindberg: A Psychoanalytic Study with Special Reference to the Oedipus Complex*. Boston: Gorham, 1920.

ACTORS, DIRECTORS, THEATER PROFESSIONALS

Anderson, Carl. "Strindberg's Translations of American Humor." *Scandinavian-American Interrelations*. Oslo: Universitetsforlaget, 1971.

Bulman, Joan. *Strindberg and Shakespeare*. London: Jonathan Cape, 1933.

Ekman, Hans-Göran. *Strindberg and the Five Senses: Studies in Strindberg's Chamber Plays*. New Brunswick, N. J.: Athlone Press, 2000.

Jaspers, Karl. *Strindberg and Van Gogh*. Tucson: University of Arizona Press, 1977.

Johannesson, Eric. *Strindberg and the Historical Drama*. Seattle: University of Washington Press, 1963.

_____. *The Novels of August Strindberg*. Berkeley and Los Angeles: University of California Press, 1968.

Lagercrantz, Olof. *August Strindberg*. London: Faber, 1984.

Lucas, F. L. *Ibsen and Strindberg*. London: Cassell, 1962.

Sprigge, Elizabeth, *The Strange Life of August Strindberg*. London: Chatto and Windus, 1949.

Sprinchorn, Evert. *Strindberg as Dramatist*. New Haven, Conn., and London: Yale University Press, 1982.

Uddgren, Gustav. *Strindberg the Man*. Boston: Four Seas, 1920.

Ward, John. *The Social and Religious Plays of Strindberg*. London: Athlone Press, 1980.

Waxman, S. M. *Antoine and the Théâtre Libre*. Cambridge, Mass.: Harvard University Press, 1926.

THE EDITIONS OF STRINDBERG'S WORKS USED FOR THIS BOOK

August Strindberg. *Five Major Plays* [*The Father, Miss Julie, The Stronger, A Dream Play, The Ghost Sonata*], translated by Carl R. Mueller. Lyme, N.H.: Smith and Kraus, 2000. [ISBN 1-57525-261-9]

_____. *Five Major Plays,* vol. II [*Playing with Fire, Creditors, The Dance of Death I & II, Storm*], translated by Carl R. Mueller. Lyme, N.H.: Smith and Kraus, 2002. [ISBN 1-57525-320-8]

SOURCES CITED IN THIS BOOK

Jacobs, Barry, and Egil Törnqvist. *Strindberg's Miss Julie: A Play and Its Transpositions*. Norwich, UK: Norvik, 1988.

Meyer, Michael. *Strindberg: A Biography*. London and New York: Secker and Warburg and Random House, 1985.

Morgan, Margery. *August Strindberg*. London: Macmillan, 1985.

INDEX

The entries in the index include highlights from the main In an Hour essay portion of the book.

ABOUT THE AUTHOR

Carl Mueller was a professor in the Department of Theater at the University of California, Los Angeles, from 1967 until his death in 2008. There he directed and taught theater history, criticism, dramatic literature, and playwriting. He was educated at Northwestern University, where he received a B.S. in English. After work in graduate English at the University of California, Berkeley, he received his M.A. in Playwriting at UCLA, where he also completed his Ph.D. in Theater History and Criticism. In 1960–1961 he was a Fulbright Scholar in Berlin.

A translator for more than forty years, he translated and published works by Büchner, Brecht, Wedekind, Hauptmann, Hofmannsthal, and Hebbel, to name a few. His published translation of von Horváth's *Tales from the Vienna Woods* was given its London West End premiere in July 1999. For Smith and Kraus he translated individual volumes of plays by Schnitzler, Strindberg, Pirandello, Kleist, and Wedekind. His translation of Goethe's *Faust Part One* and *Part Two* appeared in 2004. He also translated for Smith and Kraus *Sophokles: The Complete Plays* (2000), a two-volume *Aeschylus: The Complete Plays* (2002), and a four-volume *Euripides: The Complete Plays* (2005). His translations have been performed in every English-speaking country and have appeared on BBC-TV.

Smith and Kraus wishes to thank Hugh Denard, whose enlightened permissions policy reflects an understanding that copyright law is intended to both protect the rights of creators of intellectual property as well as to encourage its use for the public good.

Know the playwright,
love the play.

Open a new door to theater study, performance, and
audience satisfaction with these Playwrights In an Hour titles.

ANCIENT GREEK
Aeschylus   Aristophanes   Euripides   Sophocles

RENAISSANCE
William Shakespeare

MODERN
Anton Chekhov   Noël Coward   Lorraine Hansberry
Henrik Ibsen   Arthur Miller   Molière   Eugene O'Neill
Arthur Schnitzler   George Bernard Shaw   August Strindberg
Frank Wedekind   Oscar Wilde   Thornton Wilder
Tennessee Williams

CONTEMPORARY
Edward Albee   Alan Ayckbourn   Samuel Beckett
Theresa Rebeck   Sarah Ruhl   Sam Shepard   Tom Stoppard
August Wilson

To purchase or for more information
visit our web site inanhourbooks.com